The Fruit of the Holy Spirit as SPIRITUAL WARFARE
Companion Guide

Rivkah Isaacs

Treasures of Glory Ministries
San Diego, California

Copyright © 2014-2016 Rivkah Isaacs

Published by Treasures of Glory Ministries
P.O. Box 23743, San Diego, CA 92193-3743
www.treasuresofglory.com

First printing.

Printed in the United States of America.

All rights reserved. This book is protected by the copyright laws of the United States of America. No part of this publication may be reproduced, stored in a retrieval system or transmitted in any for or by any means—electronic, mechanical, photocopy, recording or any other—without the prior written permission of the publisher. The only exception is brief quotations in printed reviews.

Unless otherwise indicated, Scripture taken from the New King James Version®. Copyright © 1982 by Thomas Nelson, Inc. Used by permission. All rights reserved.

Scripture quotations taken from the Amplified® Bible, Copyright © 1954, 1958, 1962, 1964, 1965, 1987 by The Lockman Foundation. Used by permission. (www.Lockman.org)

Scripture quotations marked ESV are from The Holy Bible, English Standard Version® (ESV®), copyright © 2001 by Crossway, a publishing ministry of Good News Publishers. Used by permission. All rights reserved.

Scripture quotations marked KJV are taken from the King James Version of the Bible.

Scripture quotations taken from the New American Standard Bible®, Copyright © 1960, 1962, 1963, 1968, 1971, 1972, 1973, 1975, 1977, 1995 by The Lockman Foundation. Used by permission. (www.Lockman.org)

Scripture quotation marked NIV are taken from the HOLY BIBLE, NEW INTERNATIONAL VERSION®, NIV® Copyright © 1973, 1978, 1984, 2011 by Biblica, Inc.® Used by permission. All rights reserved worldwide.

ISBN-13: 978-0-9916112-0-1

But the fruit of the Spirit is love, joy, peace, patience, kindness, goodness, faithfulness, gentleness, self-control; against such things there is no law.
                                              Galatians 5:22-23 (ESV)

Do not be overcome by evil, but overcome evil with good.
                                              Romans 12:21

Table of Contents

SESSION 1 Introduction to the Series of the Fruit of the Holy Spirit as Spiritual Warfare 1
- **Purpose of the Series** 1
  - The Order of Removing and Replacing Strongholds 2
  - The Fruit of the Holy Spirit Is Always Relational 2
- **Roles of the Godhead** 3
  - God the Father 3
  - God the Son 3
  - God the Holy Spirit 3
- **Structure of this Series** 4

SESSION 2 Love as Spiritual Warfare—Part 1 5
- **Introduction to Love** 5
- **Love vs. Fear** 7
- **What Is Love?** 7
- **Prayer for Impartation of Love** 8

SESSION 3 Love As Spiritual Warfare—Part 2 9
- **Love: Spiritual Warfare Against Fear** 9
- **Love: Spiritual Warfare Against Control** 9
- **Love: Spiritual Warfare Against Rebellion** 9
- **Love: Spiritual Warfare Against Pride** 10
  - Pride Is Idolatry 10
- **Love: Spiritual Warfare Against the Orphan Spirit** 10
  - Characteristics of an Orphan Spirit 11
- **Love: Spiritual Warfare Against Rejection** 12
  - Characteristics of Rejection 12
- **Love: Spiritual Warfare Against Self-Hatred and Unloving** 13
  - Characteristics of Self-Hatred and Unloving Spirit 13
- **Love: Spiritual Warfare Against the Religious Spirit** 14
  - Characteristics of the Religious Spirit 14
- **Love: Spiritual Warfare Against the Legalistic Spirit** 14
  - Characteristics of the Legalistic Spirit 14
- **Love: Spiritual Warfare Against Jealousy and Envy** 15
  - Characteristics of Jealousy and Envy 15
- **Love: Spiritual Warfare Against Accusations, Gossip and Slander of Others** 16
- **Love: Spiritual Warfare Against the Spirit of Poverty** 16
- **Love: Spiritual Warfare Against Hatred** 16
  - Stages of Bitterness 16
- **Love: Spiritual Warfare Against Accusing Spirits—Toward Self and God** 17
  - Conviction vs. Accusation 17
- **Love: Spiritual Warfare Against Unbelief and Doubt** 18
  - Doubt vs. Unbelief 18
- **Where Does Doubt Reside?** 19
  - Doubt Resides in the Heart 19
  - Doubt Resides in the Mind 19
- **Where Does Unbelief Reside?** 19

  Unbelief Resides in the Heart 19
  Unbelief Resides in the Mind 19
Love: Spiritual Warfare for Healing—Inner Healing, Deliverance, Physical Healing 20
Prayers for Love 21
  General Prayer for Love 21
  Prayer for Repentance of Fear (Specific Fear-Related Sins) 21

SESSION 4 Joy as Spiritual Warfare 23
Connection of Joy and Righteousness 23
Context of Joy in Nehemiah 23
Connection of Jesus with Joy and Righteousness 23
Joy as Strength with Focus on Relationship 24
Prayer for Joy 25
  Prayer for Repentance of Unrighteousness and Impartation of Joy 25

SESSION 5 Peace as Spiritual Warfare 27
Introduction 27
Connection of Peace and Righteousness 27
Peace as Covenant with God 28
  Old Testament Examples of Peace and Righteousness 28
  New Testament Example of a Covenant of Peace 28
Peace: Spiritual Warfare for Blessings 29
  The Priestly Blessing 29
Peace: Spiritual Warfare for Healing 29
Peace: Rest as Spiritual Warfare 29
  Old Testament References Link Peace to Quietness and Rest 29
  God Rested on the Seventh Day of Creation 30
Peace: Spiritual Warfare as Rest for Sleep 30
Peace: Rest in Warfare 30
  Rest in the Middle of War 30
Old Testament Connection of Peace and Righteousness 31
New Testament Connection of Peace and Righteousness 31
  Peace on Earth 31
Peace and Righteousness as Spiritual Warfare 32
Peace: Spiritual Warfare for Evangelism 32
  Armor: Feet Shod With The Gospel of Peace 32
Peace: Spiritual Warfare Against Satan 33
  Significance of the Foot 34
Peace: Spiritual Warfare for Those Coming Out of the Occult 34
  Peace and Kingdom of God: Righteousness, Peace and Joy in the Holy Ghost 34
  Covenant of Peace 34
Peace: Spiritual Warfare in Guarding the Heart and Mind 35
Prayers for Peace 36
  Prayer for Repentance and Impartation of Peace 36
  Prayer to Break Occult Covenants/Replacement of Covenant of Peace 36

SESSION 6 The Kingdom of God: Righteousness, Peace and Joy 39
Introduction 39
Connection of Joy and Righteousness 39
Connection of Peace and Righteousness 39
  Righteousness, Peace and Joy comprise the Kingdom of God 39

    The Kingdom of God and the Connection to Peace 40
The Kingdom of God and the Connection to Righteousness... 40
    Melchizedek Described in More Detail.. 40
    The Kingdom of God Relates to Righteousness and Peace 40
    Jesus' Connection to Ruling in Peace and Righteousness 40

SESSION 7 Patience as Spiritual Warfare 43
Introduction.. 43
    Definition of Patience 43
    Patience vs. Self-Control 44
Patience: Spiritual Warfare for Unity 44
    God of Patience and Comfort... 44
Patience and Unity: Spiritual Warfare for Favor and Redemption 45
    Steps to Gain Favor in Acts 2:46-47 46
Patience: Spiritual Warfare as We Wait for Coming of the Lord............................. 46
Patience: Spiritual Warfare for Endurance 47
The Purpose of Patience Is Unity... 47
Prayer for Patience 48
    Prayer for Repentance and Impartation of Patience 48

SESSION 8 Kindness as Spiritual Warfare 49
Kindness: Spiritual Warfare for Repentance.. 49
Link Between Repentance and Redemption 49
Kindness: Spiritual Warfare for Redemption.. 50
    Law of the Kinsman-Redeemer (Leviticus 25:23-28) 50
    The Levirate Marriage 51
    Kindness in the Book of Ruth 51
Kindness: Connection to Redemption and Mercy 52
    Covenant of Peace 52
Kindness: Spiritual Warfare for Evangelism 52
Kindness: Spiritual Warfare Against Grieving the Holy Spirit 53
Kindness: Spiritual Warfare Against Judgment and for Repentance—Initial Repentance and Continual Repentance 53
Prayer for Kindness 55
    Kindness: Repentance Prayer and Prayer for Impartation 55

SESSION 9 Goodness as Spiritual Warfare 57
Introduction.. 57
    Definition of Goodness in Scripture 57
Goodness: Justice as Spiritual Warfare 58
    Goodness and Justice 58
    Justice Involves Restoration and Restitution 59
    Joseph is a Biblical Example of Justice, Restoration and Restitution 59
    Justice Gives Identity, Protection and Provision.. 59
Goodness: Mercy as Spiritual Warfare 60
Mercy Triumphs Over Judgment 60
Goodness and Mercy: Spiritual Warfare Against Judgment and Guilt 60
Goodness: Humility as Spiritual Warfare 61
Goodness and Glory: Spiritual Warfare Over the Spirit of Leviathan (Pride) 61
God's Glory Is His Goodness 61
Goodness: Glory as Spiritual Warfare.. 61

The Goodness of God Satisfies as Spiritual Warfare 63
What Does Satan Use to Attack God's Goodness? 63
Prayers for Goodness 65
Goodness: Repentance Prayer and Prayer of Impartation 65
Prayer for Justice, Restoration and Restitution 65

SESSION 10 Goodness and Mercy—Spiritual Warfare Against Judgment and Guilt 67
What Is Guilt? 67
What Is Judgment? 67
Judgment vs. Discernment 68
Discernment 68
Judgment 68
Mercy Triumphs Over Judgment 68
Mercy Is Found in God's Goodness 69
Guilt Producers 69
Freedom from Guilt 70
Prayers for Goodness and Mercy 72
Prayer to Repent for Judging Self and Others (Freedom from Guilt) 72
Prayer to Forgive Others for Judgment Toward You (Freedom from Guilt) 72
Prayer for Impartation of Mercy 73

SESSION 11 Goodness and Glory as Spiritual Warfare Against the Spirit of Leviathan 75
Introduction 75
Leviathan 75
References of Leviathan as a Natural and Physical Being 75
References of Leviathan as a Spiritual Being 75
Scripture Linking Physical and Spiritual Aspects of Leviathan 76
Job 41 76
Glory and Goodness: Spiritual Warfare Against Leviathan 82
Glory as Spiritual Warfare 82
Goodness and Glory in Relationship to the Armor of God 82
Connecting Goodness, Glory and the Fruit of the Holy Spirit as Spiritual Warfare Against Leviathan 82
God Is the One Who Will Defeat Leviathan 83
Prayer for Goodness and Glory 84
Prayer for Repentance of Spirit of Leviathan and Impartation of Goodness and Glory ... 84

SESSION 12 Faith as Spiritual Warfare 87
Introduction 87
Questions Answered in This Session 87
Definition of Faith 87
Faith: Spiritual Warfare Against Unbelief 88
Strongholds of Unbelief and Soul Wounds That Hold Unbelief in Place 89
Faith: Spiritual Warfare for Physical Healing and Freedom from Demonic Torment 90
Faith in Christ: Spiritual Warfare for Miracles 90
Faith Can Bring Blessings That Were Not Intended for Us 91
Gentile Mother 91
King Hezekiah 91

- **Faith: Spiritual Warfare for Peace** 91
- **Faith: Spiritual Warfare as Reminder of Utter Destruction of the Enemy** 92
- **Faith: Spiritual Warfare Against the Spirit of Poverty** 93
- **Faith: Belief in God vs. Turning His Promises into Idols** 94
- **Prayers for Faith** 96
  - Prayer to Break Unbelief 96
  - Prayer for Healing of Soul Wounds and the Heart of Unbelief 96
  - Prayer to Renounce Unbelief 97
  - Prayer to Overcome Spirit of Poverty with Faith 97
  - Prayer to Repent for Turning God's Promises Into Idols 98

SESSION 13 Gentleness as Spiritual Warfare 99
- **Gentleness** 99
  - Satan's Opposition to Gentleness 99
  - Humility Focuses on Relationship Rather Than the Need to be Right 100
- **Gentleness Imparts Greatness** 101
- **Gentleness: Spiritual Warfare Against Anger and Pride** 102
  - Lucifer and Anger 102
  - Lucifer and Pride 102
- **Gentleness: Spiritual Warfare Against Self-Hatred and Unloving** 103
- **Gentleness: Spiritual Warfare for Correction and Restoration** 103
- **Gentleness: Spiritual Warfare for Coming into Our Inheritance** 103
  - How Does Gentleness Lead Us to Our Inheritance? 104
- **Gentleness: Spiritual Warfare for Protecting the Family** 105
  - Role of Mothers and Gentleness 105
  - Underestimating the Importance of Gentleness 105
  - Role of Fathers and Gentleness 105
- **Gentleness: Spiritual Warfare Against the Spirit of Poverty** 105
  - Gentleness Is Strategic in Overcoming the Spirit of Poverty 106
- **How Do We Act in Gentleness?** 107
- **Prayers for Gentleness** 108
  - Prayer of Repentance for Anger and Impartation of Gentleness 108
  - Prayer of Repentance for Pride and Impartation of Gentleness and Humility 108
  - Prayer to Break the Spirit of Poverty 109

SESSION 14 Self-Control as Spiritual Warfare 111
- **Introduction** 111
- **Self-Control as Spiritual Warfare** 111
- **Self-Control: Spiritual Warfare Against "As in the Days of Noah"** 112
- **History of the Nephilim Before the Flood** 112
- **History of the Nephilim After the Flood** 113
  - Noah and His Family 113
- **Connection of Jesus' Reference to the Days of Noah and Self-Control** 114
- **Self-Control: Spiritual Warfare Against Spirit of Poverty** 115
  - What Are Some Causes for Indebtedness? 115
- **Prayers for Self-Control** 117
  - Prayer to Break Areas of Bondages 117
  - Prayer for Repentance of Lack of Self-Control and Impartation of Self-Control 117
  - Prayer to Break the Curse of the Spirit of Poverty 118
- **Notes** 119

SESSION 1
Introduction to the Series of the Fruit of the Holy Spirit as Spiritual Warfare

Purpose of the Series

We need to learn to execute warfare against the Enemy by coming in the opposite spirit against his attacks.

Romans 12:21:[1]
Do not be overcome by evil, but overcome evil with good.

We need to be aware Satan attacks and accuses every aspect of the nature and character of God.

Satan's weapons (not all-inclusive):

- Anger, bitterness, fear, jealousy, envy, confusion, Spirit of Poverty, rejection, lust, lies, deception, murder, accusation, judging, etc.

God's weapons (not all-inclusive):

- Love, Joy, Peace, Patience, Kindness, Goodness, Faithfulness, Gentleness, Self-Control, the armor, truth, wisdom, understanding, Mercy, grace, glory, etc.

Examples of the Enemy's attacks against the nature of God:

- Anger opposes Love and Gentleness

- Judgment as condemnation opposes Goodness and Mercy

We need to use the Fruit of the Holy Spirit as replacements in our lives when we remove anger, rejection, fear, generational curses, etc. from our lives.

Luke 11:24-26:
"When an unclean spirit goes out of a man, he goes through dry places, seeking rest; and finding none, he says, 'I will return to my house from which I came.' And when he comes, he finds it swept and put in order. Then he goes and takes with him seven other spirits more wicked than himself, and they enter and dwell there; and the last state of that man is worse than the first."

The Order of Removing and Replacing Strongholds

2 Corinthians 10:1-6:
Now I, Paul, myself am pleading with you by the meekness and gentleness of Christ—who in presence am lowly among you, but being absent am bold toward you. But I beg you that when I am present I may not be bold with that confidence by which I intend to be bold against some, who think of us as if we walked according to the flesh. For though we walk in the flesh, we do not war according to the flesh. For the weapons of our warfare are not carnal but mighty in God for pulling down strongholds, casting down arguments and every high thing that exalts itself against the knowledge of God, bringing every thought into captivity to the obedience of Christ, and being ready to punish all disobedience when your obedience is fulfilled.

Steps to Bondage

Step 1: Temptation (dwelling on this leads to step 2)
Step 2: Sinning and practicing the act (repenting goes up to step 1, continuing leads to step 3)
Step 3: Habit (repenting goes up to step 2, continuing leads to step 4)
Step 4: Bondage (repenting goes up to step 3, continuing remains at step 4)[2]

To obtain freedom, we work through the steps backward. To grow in our freedom, we need to know what treasures exist in the Fruit of the Holy Spirit the Enemy wants to steal from us. For example, Gentleness—which contains no bitterness—leads us to greatness and brings forth inheritance. Therefore, Satan's weapon of anger destroys Gentleness because he wants to undermine our greatness and inheritance.

Another example is when we come into agreement with the Enemy to judge others, we attack God's Goodness and Mercy. In addition, we come against the work of Jesus' death and resurrection.

The Fruit of the Holy Spirit Is Always Relational

The Fruit of the Holy Spirit is heart knowledge in relationship with the Father, the Son, and the Holy Spirit and is not relegated to head knowledge.

1 John 4:18:
There is no fear in love; but perfect love casts out fear, because fear involves torment. But he who fears has not been made perfect in love.

Psalm 119:11:
*Your word I have hidden in my heart,
That I might not sin against You.*

The Holy Spirit establishes the Fruit of the Holy Spirit in our lives.

> **John 16:13-15:**
> *"However, when He, the Spirit of truth, has come, He will guide you into all truth; for He will not speak on His own authority, but whatever He hears He will speak; and He will tell you things to come. He will glorify Me, for He will take of what is Mine and declare it to you. All things that the Father has are Mine. Therefore I said that He will take of Mine and declare it to you."*

The embodiment of the Fruit of the Holy Spirit comes through intimacy and unity with the Father and Son through the Holy Spirit.

> **John 17:20-25**

Roles of the Godhead

God the Father

- Identity
- Protection
- Provision

God the Son

- Companionship
- Communication

God the Holy Spirit

- Comfort
- Nurture
- Teach[3]

2 Corinthians 13:14 (AMP):
The grace (favor and spiritual blessing) of the Lord Jesus Christ and the love of God and the presence and fellowship (the communion and sharing together, and participation) in the Holy Spirit be with you all. Amen (so be it).

Structure of this Series

Each session focuses on one aspect of the Fruit of the Holy Spirit, which are compartmentalized for the sake of simplification of the topics. In reality, they are intimately intertwined and cannot be separated from each other. The Fruit of the Holy Spirit *is* Love, Joy, Peace, etc.—not the Fruit of the Holy Spirit *are*.

This series includes examples of how to use the Fruit of the Holy Spirit in spiritual warfare. It is by no means exhaustive. My prayer for you in this series is for the Holy Spirit to open your understanding to additional ways the Fruit of the Holy Spirit can be used as spiritual warfare.

The close of each session contains prayers to remove areas from our lives where we agree with the Enemy. Any time we agree with the Enemy in opposition to the truth and nature and character of God, we sin. The prayers lead us to replace the sin we removed with an impartation to receive of the nature of God revealed to us in Fruit of the Holy Spirit.

These prayers are examples—not formulas. Remember, the Holy Spirit reveals the Fruit of the Holy Spirit through relationship.

SESSION 2
Love as Spiritual Warfare—Part 1

Introduction to Love

Deuteronomy 6:5:
"You shall love the LORD your God with all your heart, with all your soul, and with all your strength."

➤ **Definition of "heart" (Hebrew):** "heart; inner man, mind, will, heart, soul, understanding; mind, knowledge, thinking, reflection, memory; as seat of emotions and passions"

➤ **Definition of "soul" (Hebrew):** "soul, self, life, creature, person, appetite, mind, living being, desire, emotion, and passion"

Mark 12:30:
"And you shall love the LORD your God with all your heart, with all your soul, with all your mind, and with all your strength.' This is the first commandment."

➤ **Definition of "heart: (Greek):** "the heart; the soul or mind, as it is the fountain and seat of the thoughts, passions, desires, appetites, affections, purposes and endeavours"

➤ **Definition of "soul" (Greek):** "the soul; the seat of the feelings, desires, affections and aversions (our heart, soul, etc.)"

Psalm 27

1 John 1:1-4:
That which was from the beginning, which we have heard, which we have seen with our eyes, which we have looked upon, and our hands have handled, concerning the Word of life—the life was manifested, and we have seen, and bear witness, and declare to you that eternal life which was with the Father and was manifested to us—that which we have seen and heard we declare to you, that you also may have fellowship with us; and truly our fellowship is with the Father and with His Son Jesus Christ. And these things we write to you that your joy may be full.

1 John 4:7-21:

Beloved, let us love one another, for love is of God; and everyone who loves is born of God and knows God. He who does not love does not know God, for God is love. In this the love of God was manifested toward us, that God has sent His only begotten Son into the world, that we might live through Him. In this is love, not that we loved God, but that He loved us and sent His Son to be the propitiation for our sins. Beloved, if God so loved us, we also ought to love one another.

No one has seen God at any time. If we love one another, God abides in us, and His love has been perfected in us. By this we know that we abide in Him, and He in us, because He has given us of His Spirit. And we have seen and testify that the Father has sent the Son as Savior of the world. Whoever confesses that Jesus is the Son of God, God abides in him, and he in God. And we have known and believed the love that God has for us. God is love, and he who abides in love abides in God, and God in him.

Love has been perfected among us in this: that we may have boldness in the day of judgment; because as He is, so are we in this world. There is no fear in love; but perfect love casts out fear, because fear involves torment. But he who fears has not been made perfect in love. We love Him because He first loved us.

If someone says, "I love God," and hates his brother, he is a liar; for he who does not love his brother whom he has seen, how can he love God whom he has not seen? And this commandment we have from Him: that he who loves God must love his brother also.

1 John 5:1-5:

Whoever believes that Jesus is the Christ is born of God, and everyone who loves Him who begot also loves him who is begotten of Him. By this we know that we love the children of God, when we love God and keep His commandments. For this is the love of God, that we keep His commandments. And His commandments are not burdensome. For whatever is born of God overcomes the world. And this is the victory that has overcome the world—our faith. Who is he who overcomes the world, but he who believes that Jesus is the Son of God?

Notes:

Love vs. Fear

Scientific research proves there are two root emotions—love and fear. Every positive emotion comes from Love—Joy, Peace, Patience, Kindness, etc. Every negative emotion comes from fear—anger, self-pity, jealousy, etc.[4]

James 1:2-8:
My brethren, count it all joy when you fall into various trials, knowing that the testing of your faith produces patience. But let patience have its perfect work, that you may be perfect and complete, lacking nothing. If any of you lacks wisdom, let him ask of God, who gives to all liberally and without reproach, and it will be given to him. But let him ask in faith, with no doubting, for he who doubts is like a wave of the sea driven and tossed by the wind. For let not that man suppose that he will receive anything from the Lord; he is a double-minded man, unstable in all his ways.

Ruth 2:8-13

- Instead of saying, "and have spoken kindly to your maidservant," the Hebrew Interlinear Bible reveals that Ruth's words to Boaz reflect that he spoke on her heart.[5]

What Is Love?

Love isn't a "what." Love doesn't originate as a thought or an emotion. Love is a "Who." Love is a Person. God is Love.

Notes:

Prayer for Impartation of Love

Dear Heavenly Father, I come to You and desire to see Your beauty and to feel Your beauty in my heart. I seek Your face with my heart. I desire to feel Your Love for me, to experience it in my heart and not to only know with my mind. Please speak kindly on my heart. I long to feel Your Love ever present in the depths of my heart. I desire to love You with my heart, my inner man, mind, will, soul, understanding, knowledge, thoughts, reflection, memory and with my heart, which is the seat of emotions and passions. I desire to love You with all my emotions and my passions. Please reveal in me any emotions, hurts, trauma, etc. that are not rooted in Love. I give them to You to heal. Please bring Your perfect and complete healing to my heart, mind and emotions. Through the power of the Holy Spirit, please show me Your tangible Love each day. May I know Your heart more intimately. I give You all fear. Please speak to me about Your Perfect Love for me. I desire to know Your Love with my entire being. I no longer want to have Your Love be relegated to my mind. I receive Your Love for me with all that I am. Father, please show me the identity You have for me. Please show me how You protect and provide for me. In Jesus' name, amen. (Please, take time to receive and rest in the Love of your Heavenly Father.)

Dear Jesus, I thank You for preparing me for the Marriage Supper of the Lamb. I am to be Your bride. Since we are to spend eternity together, I desire to know how to be loved by You and how to love You. Please show me how to communicate with You and how to live in companionship with You. I desire to feel Your Love more deeply in my heart. I need to know Your precious Love for me with all that is in me. In knowing Your Love for me, I will be able to love others as You love them. Please transform my life with Your Love so that I can bring others in closer relationship with You. You are beautiful. Thank You for Your selfless Love for me. Please speak to my heart about Your Love for me. Amen. (Please, take time to allow Jesus to share His heart with you.)

Dear Holy Spirit, thank You that I can know the Love of the Father and the Love of Jesus through You. Please teach me about Perfect Love and how to receive it. Please reveal the Heart of the Father to me and transform my nature into God's nature of Love. I thank You for Your comfort and nurture in my life. I know that these aspects of Your nature are essential for me to experience the Love of the Father. Please reveal truth to me about Your Love. In Jesus' name, amen. (Please, take time to let the Holy Spirit minister to your heart.)

SESSION 3
Love As Spiritual Warfare—Part 2

Love: Spiritual Warfare Against Fear

Romans 8:15:
For you did not receive the spirit of bondage again to fear, but you received the Spirit of adoption by whom we cry out, "Abba, Father."

I John 4:18-19:
There is no fear in love; but perfect love casts out fear, because fear involves torment. But he who fears has not been made perfect in love. We love because He first loved us.

Fear attacks the Love of the Father.

Fear comes against the role of the Father to give identity, protection and provision.

Love: Spiritual Warfare Against Control

Control is based in fear.

Control is witchcraft.

Love: Spiritual Warfare Against Rebellion

John 14:23-24:
Jesus answered and said to him, "If anyone loves Me, he will keep My word; and My Father will love him, and We will come to him and make Our home with him. He who does not love Me does not keep My words; and the word which you hear is not Mine but the Father's who sent Me."

1 Samuel 15:23:
*"For rebellion is as the sin of witchcraft,
And stubbornness is as iniquity and idolatry."*

Love: Spiritual Warfare Against Pride

1 Corinthians 13:4-7:
Love suffers long and is kind; love does not envy; love does not parade itself, is not puffed up; does not behave rudely, does not seek its own, is not provoked, thinks no evil; does not rejoice in iniquity, but rejoices in the truth; bears all things, believes all things, hopes all things, endures all things.

1 Corinthians 13:13:
And now abide faith, hope, love, these three; but the greatest of these is love.

Satan's pride brought about rebellion among the angels in heaven.

Isaiah 14:12-17

Pride Is Idolatry

The First Commandment

Exodus 20:3:
"You shall have no other gods before Me."

The Second Commandment

Exodus 20:4-6

Love: Spiritual Warfare Against the Orphan Spirit

Romans 8:15-17:
For you did not receive the spirit of bondage again to fear, but you received the Spirit of adoption by whom we cry out, "Abba, Father." The Spirit Himself bears witness with our spirit that we are children of God, and if children, then heirs—heirs of God and joint heirs with Christ, if indeed we suffer with Him, that we may also be glorified.

Characteristics of an Orphan Spirit

- Lives life from a place of not feeling safe and secure in the Father's heart
- Feels parentless with an inability to relate to the father of the family
- Does not feel affirmation
- Does not feel protected
- Has no sense of belonging
- Is not comforted
- Is lonely or has a loner spirit (person who prefers to be alone)
- Suffers from loneliness and feels alone even among family and friends
- Feels rejection or finds it easy to feel rejected or unwanted
- Has an inability to bond with people
- Seems incapable of trusting people
- Is inwardly isolated
- Has no one from whom to draw Godly inheritance
- Leads to striving to achieve, compete and earn everything
- Lives a life of anxiety, fears and frustration
- Results in a wandering spirit—feels like no place is home
- Is insecure and unsure of other's feelings
- Lives *for* Love and not *from* Love
- Mistakenly thinks that repentance is based on thoughts of punishment, loss and unworthiness
- Labors under a performance mentality
- Gravitates toward rebellion or a Religious Spirit
- Is jealous and envious

Notes:

Love: Spiritual Warfare Against Rejection

Rejection is rooted in the Orphan Spirit.

Romans 8:15-17

Characteristics of Rejection

- Abandonment
- Accusation by others
- Control and manipulation
- Deep hurt and wounded spirit
- Depression
- Discontentment
- Double-minded
- Fabricated personality
- False burden-bearing
- False responsibility
- Fear of abandonment
- Fear of deliverance
- Fear of failure
- Fear of man
- Fear of rejection
- Fear of vulnerability
- Insecurity
- Lust and fantasy lust
- Need for acceptance
- Need for approval
- Need for identity
- Need for love
- Rebellion
- Rejection by others
- Rejection of others
- Self-accusation
- Self-hatred
- Self-pity
- Self-rejection
- Ungrateful[6]

Notes:

Love: Spiritual Warfare Against Self-Hatred and Unloving

Self-Hatred and unloving are rooted in the Orphan Spirit.

Characteristics of Self-Hatred and Unloving Spirit

- Addictions
- Adultery
- Anorexia
- Attention-getting
- Broken heart
- Bulimia
- Competition
- Compulsiveness
- Division
- Double-minded
- Drunkenness
- Excessive talking
- Fabricated personality
- False piety
- Fornication
- I and I will
- Insecurity
- Isolation
- Lack of confidence
- Loneliness
- Need for approval
- Perfectionism
- Pornography
- Programming
- Religious Spirit
- Self-abasement
- Self-accusation
- Self-anger
- Self-bitterness
- Self-comparison
- Self-condemnation
- Self-deception
- Self-doubt
- Self-exaltation
- Self-hatred
- Self-Idolatry
- Self-murder
- Self-mutilation
- Self-pity
- Self-questioning
- Self-rejection
- Self-resentment
- Self-sabotage
- Self-torment
- Self-unforgiveness
- Self-violence
- Selfishness
- Separation
- Shame
- Victimization[7]

Notes:

Love: Spiritual Warfare Against the Religious Spirit

The Religious Spirit is rooted in the Orphan Spirit.

> ➤ **Definition of "religious spirit":** "seeks religious activity as a substitute for the power of the Holy Spirit"[8]

Characteristics of the Religious Spirit

- Critical
- Judgmental
- Perfectionist

Love: Spiritual Warfare Against the Legalistic Spirit

The Legalistic Spirit is rooted in the Orphan Spirit.

> ➤ **Definition of "legalism":** "is a usually pejorative term referring to an over-emphasis on discipline of conduct or legal ideas, usually implying an allegation of misguided rigor, pride, superficiality, neglect of mercy, and ignorance of the grace of God or emphasizing the letter of law at the expense of the spirit [of the law]"[9]

Characteristics of the Legalistic Spirit

- Has no mercy for transgressions
- Judgmental
- Strict concerning the law

Notes:

Love: Spiritual Warfare Against Jealousy and Envy

Jealousy and envy are rooted in the Orphan Spirit.

> **Romans 12:15-16a:**
> *Rejoice with those who rejoice, mourn with those who mourn. Be of the same mind toward one another.*

- **Definition of "jealousy" (Webster):** "That passion of peculiar uneasiness which arises from the fear that a rival may rob us of the affection of one whom we love, or the suspicion that he has already done it; or it is the uneasiness which arises from the fear that another does or will enjoy some advantage which we desire for ourselves. A man's jealousy is excited by the attentions of a rival to his favorite lady. A woman's jealousy is roused by her husband's attentions to another woman. In short, jealousy is awakened by whatever may exalt others, or give them pleasures and advantages that we desire for ourselves. Jealousy is nearly allied to envy, for jealousy, before a good is lost by ourselves, is converted into envy, after it is obtained by others."[10]

Characteristics of Jealousy and Envy

- Anger
- Comparison
- Competition
- Control
- Covetousness
- Critical spirits
- Curse of touching God's anointed
- Discontent
- Envy
- Fear
- Fear of loss of control
- Gossip
- Hatred
- Idolatry
- Jealousy
- Jealousy (spouse-related)
- Murder
- Not trusting God
- Possessiveness
- Pride
- Resentment
- Retaliation
- Rivalry
- Self-ambition
- Strife
- Superiority
- Unbelief God will provide
- Unforgiveness
- Violence[11]

Notes:

Love: Spiritual Warfare Against Accusations, Gossip and Slander of Others

Accusations, gossip and slander are rooted in jealousy and envy. Jealousy and envy are rooted in the Orphan Spirit.

Matthew 12:34b:
"For out of the abundance of the mouth the heart speaks."

Love: Spiritual Warfare Against the Spirit of Poverty

The Spirit of Poverty is rooted in the Orphan Spirit.

Ephesians 3:8-21

- **Definition of "poverty" (Isaacs):** "living in lack, or living without something that is established for us through the finished work of the Cross, and experiencing anything that is less than the fullness of our inheritance"

Love: Spiritual Warfare Against Hatred

Matthew 5:43-48

Stages of Bitterness

In order of severity:
1. Unforgiveness
2. Resentment
3. Retaliation
4. Anger
5. Hatred
6. Violence
7. Murder

Isaiah 43:25:
"I, even I, am He who blots out your transgressions for My own sake, And I will not remember your sins."

I John 4:19-21:
We love Him because He first loved us.

If someone says, "I love God," and hates his brother, he is a liar; for he who does not love his brother whom he has seen, how can he love God whom he has not seen? And this commandment we have from Him: that he who loves God must love his brother also.

Love: Spiritual Warfare Against Accusing Spirits—Toward Self and God

John 10:27:
"My sheep listen to my voice, and I know them, and they follow me."

Psalm 119:41-42 (NASB):
May Your lovingkindnesses also come to me, O LORD,
Your salvation according to Your word;
So I will have an answer for him who reproaches me,
For I trust in Your word.

Conviction vs. Accusation

Revelation 12:10:
Then I heard a loud voice saying in heaven, "Now salvation, and strength, and the kingdom of our God, and the power of His Christ have come, for the accuser of our brethren, who accused them before our God day and night, has been cast down."

John 16:5-11

Notes:

Love: Spiritual Warfare Against Unbelief and Doubt

Doubt vs. Unbelief

- **Definition of "doubt" (Greek):**
  1) "to separate, make a distinction, discriminate, to prefer
  2) to learn by discrimination, to try, decide
     a) to determine, give judgment, decide a dispute
  3) to withdraw from one, desert
  4) to separate oneself in a hostile spirit, to oppose, strive with dispute, contend
  5) to be at variance with oneself, hesitate, doubt"

- **Definition of "doubt" (Webster):**
  1) "to waver or fluctuate in opinion; to hesitate; to be in suspense; to be in uncertainty, respecting the truth or fact; to be undetermined
  2) to fear; to be apprehensive; to suspect"[12]

- **Definition of "doubt" (Wikipedia):** "doubt, a status between belief and disbelief, involves uncertainty, or distrust or lack of sureness of an alleged fact, an action, a motive or decision"[13]

- **Definition of "unbelief" (Hebrew):** "weakness of faith"

- **Definition of "belief" (Hebrew):** "to think to be true, to be persuaded of, to credit, place confidence in; of the thing believed; in a moral or religious reference; to trust in Jesus or God as able to aid either in obtaining or in doing something: saving faith"

Example of Unbelief (Not Believing)

Matthew 13:58:
Now He did not do many mighty works there because of their unbelief.

Example Unbelief as Weakness of Faith

Mark 9:24:
Immediately the father of the child cried out and said with tears, "Lord, I believe; help my unbelief!"

Example of Doubt

James 1:6-8:
But let him ask in faith, with no doubting, for he who doubts is like a wave of the sea driven and tossed by the wind. For let not that man suppose that he will receive anything from the Lord; he is a double-minded man, unstable in all his ways.

Where Does Doubt Reside?

Doubt Resides in the Heart

Mark 11:22-24

Doubt Resides in the Mind

James 1:6-8

➢ **Definition of "doubt" (Greek):** "to separate, make a distinction, decide and to determine"

Where Does Unbelief Reside?

Unbelief Resides in the Heart

Luke 24:25-27

On the road to Emmaus, Jesus said to the two He was traveling with that they were "slow of heart to believe" the words of the prophets.

Unbelief Resides in the Mind

By definition of the word "believe," it shows it resides in the mind. The most common word in Greek for "believe" means to "think to be true."

Unbelief and doubt both have like-minded spirits that hold them in place. They don't work alone.

Love: Spiritual Warfare for Healing—Inner Healing, Deliverance, Physical Healing

Matthew 14:14:
And when Jesus went out He saw a great multitude; and He was moved with compassion for them, and healed their sick.

Notes:

Prayers for Love

General Prayer for Love

Dear Heavenly Father, in the name of the Lord Jesus Christ, I repent for not loving You with all my heart, soul, mind and strength. I recognize that in the areas of my heart, mind and soul where fear, unforgiveness, resentment, retaliation, anger, hatred, violence, murder, trauma, rejection, judgment, rebellion, self-hatred, jealousy, envy, perfectionism, the Orphan Spirit, the Spirit of Poverty and control exist, I cannot love You with those areas. Each of these destructive emotions gives a foothold to unbelief. Please forgive me for fear and all the emotions that stem from fear that reside in my heart, soul and mind. I also forgive myself. I repent on behalf of all my generations on both sides of my family line. I ask Your forgiveness for fear and all fear-based emotions and behavior; for unbelief and for not loving You with all our heart, soul, mind and strength. I bind and break all of Satan's power and authority in my life and in all my generations from not loving You with all our heart, soul, mind and strength. I renounce agreement that Love is a decision and not an emotion. I believe that You are Love. You desire my heart to be healed so I can feel Your Love toward me. Please help me to love You with everything I am. Father, please teach me how to receive Your Love through the Scriptures, and through intimate relationship with You, Your Son Jesus and Your Holy Spirit. In Jesus' name, amen.

Prayer for Repentance of Fear (Specific Fear-Related Sins)

Dear Heavenly Father, in the name of the Lord Jesus Christ, I recognize I have sinned by agreeing with (fear, unforgiveness, etc.). I take responsibility for (list the sin) and I repent. Please forgive me, and I forgive myself. I renounce agreement with this sin and I choose to change the way I think about this sin. I also repent and ask for forgiveness for the unbelief that was connected to this sin. I bind and break all of Satan's power and authority over me in this area of my life. I repent and ask forgiveness for any way my generations also committed this sin in their lives, back to Adam and Eve on both sides of my family line. I bind and break all of Satan's power and authority over me in all my generations in the area of this sin. Through the power of the Holy Spirit, please replace it with Your Love, Joy, Peace and Gentleness. Please teach me how to live in freedom and righteousness through Your Word, through the Holy Spirit, and through intimacy with You. Through the power of the Holy Spirit and through Your glory, please heal me from the effects of this sin in my body, mind, thoughts, will, heart, emotions, passions and desires. In Jesus' name, amen.

(See Session 2 for the prayer for the impartation of Love.)

SESSION 4
Joy as Spiritual Warfare

Connection of Joy and Righteousness

- **Definition of "joy" (Hebrew and Greek):** "joy, gladness"

- **Definition of "joy" (Webster):**
  1) "a: the emotion evoked by well-being, success, or good fortune or by the prospect of possessing what one desires: DELIGHT
     b: the expression or exhibition of such emotion: GAIETY
  2) a state of happiness or felicity: BLISS
  3) a source or cause of delight"[14]

- **Definition of "glad" (Webster):**
  1) "*archaic*: having a cheerful or happy disposition by nature
  2) experiencing pleasure, joy, or delight: made happy"[15]

  Nehemiah 8:10b:
  "…for the joy of the LORD is your strength."

  Philippians 4:13:
  I can do all things through Christ who strengthens me.

Context of Joy in Nehemiah

Nehemiah 8:1-10

Connection of Jesus with Joy and Righteousness

Hebrews 12:1-2

Jesus was filled with Joy to live a righteous life so that He could be the spotless Lamb of God for the ultimate purpose of righteousness—to make us righteous.

The example of Jesus enduring the Cross and despising its shame is the ultimate spiritual warfare.

Revelation 1:18:
"I am He who lives, and was dead, and behold, I am alive forevermore. Amen. And I have the keys of Hades and of Death."

Joy as Strength with Focus on Relationship

James 1:2-4:
My brethren, count it all joy when you fall into various trials, knowing that the testing of your faith produces patience. But let patience have its perfect work, that you may be perfect and complete, lacking nothing.

Focus on the Joy needed for righteousness to produce Patience.

1 Thessalonians 5:16-18:
Rejoice always, pray without ceasing, in everything give thanks; for this is the will of God in Christ Jesus for you.

- ➤ **Definition of "rejoice" (Greek):** "to rejoice, be glad; to rejoice exceedingly; to be well and thrive"

Notes:

Prayer for Joy

Prayer for Repentance of Unrighteousness and Impartation of Joy

Dear Heavenly Father, in the name of the Lord Jesus Christ, I recognize I have had a limited understanding of Joy. I repent of restricting Joy to having strength to get my "to-do" list completed, focusing on accomplishing the tasks at hand and not focusing on living righteously. I repent of not living righteously. Please forgive me. I forgive myself. I change the way I think about Joy. I choose to replace my thinking with the truth that Joy is to give me strength to live righteously. I bind and break Satan's power and authority over me in the area of focusing on things instead of focusing on living in right relationship with You, myself and others. I ask You to forgive my generations back to Adam and Eve for focusing on doing things instead of focusing on righteousness. I declare that Satan's power and authority over the area of unrighteousness in my generations is broken. I renounce agreement with unrighteousness.

Heavenly Father, through the power of the Holy Spirit, please place in me Your Joy for strength to live righteously in all that I am. I thank You that I can do all things through Christ who gives me strength. I know if I do all things right, but do not have Love, I am nothing. I receive Your Joy for the strength to live righteously in Love. Please teach me how to live with Joy and righteousness through Your Word, through the Holy Spirit and through intimacy with You. Thank You that Joy is necessary in trials, and through the testing of my Faith, Joy produces Patience. Thank You that the result of the perfect work of Patience is that I may be perfect and complete, lacking nothing. Please bring justice, restoration and restitution into my life where Joy was stolen from me by the Enemy. In Jesus' name, amen.

SESSION 5
Peace as Spiritual Warfare

Introduction

Psalm 85:10 (NIV):
Love and faithfulness meet together; righteousness and peace kiss each other.

Romans 16:20 (NIV):
The God of peace will soon crush Satan under your feet.

Isaiah 48:22:
"There is no peace," says the LORD, "for the wicked."

Connection of Peace and Righteousness

The Old Testament and New Testament connections of Peace and Righteousness

- **Definition of "peace"—*shalom* (Hebrew):**
    1) "completeness, soundness, welfare, peace
        a) completeness (in number)
        b) safety, soundness (in body)
        c) welfare, health, prosperity
        d) peace, quiet, tranquility, contentment
        e) peace, friendship
            i) of human relationships
            ii) with God especially in covenant relationship
        f) peace (from war)
        g) peace (as adjective)"

- **Definition of "peace"—Galatians 5:22—(Greek):**
    1) "a state of national tranquility
        a) exemption from the rage and havoc of war
    2) peace between individuals, i.e. harmony, concord
    3) security, safety, prosperity, felicity, (because peace and harmony make and keep things safe and prosperous)
    4) of the Messiah's peace
    5) the way that leads to peace (salvation)
    6) of Christianity, the tranquil state of a soul assured of its salvation through Christ, and so fearing nothing from God and content with its earthly lot, of whatsoever sort that is
    7) the blessed state of devout and upright men after death"

Peace as Covenant with God

Old Testament Examples of Peace and Righteousness

Numbers 25:12:
"Therefore say, 'Behold, I give to him My covenant of peace.'"

Ezekiel 37:26-28:
"'"Moreover I will make a covenant of peace with them, and it shall be an everlasting covenant with them; I will establish them and multiply them, and I will set My sanctuary in their midst forevermore. My tabernacle shall also be with them; indeed I will be their God, and they shall be My people. Then the nations will know that I, the LORD, sanctify Israel, when My sanctuary is in their midst forevermore."'"

Malachi 2:4-7:
*"Then you shall know that I have sent this commandment to you,
That My covenant with Levi may continue,"
Says the LORD of hosts.
"My covenant was with him, one of life and peace,
And I gave them to him that he might fear Me;
So he feared Me
And was reverent before My name.
The law of truth was in his mouth,
And injustice was not found on his lips.
He walked with Me in peace and equity,
And turned many away from iniquity.*

*"For the lips of a priest should keep knowledge,
And people should seek the law from his mouth;
For he is the messenger of the LORD of hosts."*

Isaiah 48:22:
"There is no peace," says the LORD, "for the wicked."

New Testament Example of a Covenant of Peace

John 14:26-28:
"But the Helper, the Holy Spirit, whom the Father will send in My name, He will teach you all things, and bring to your remembrance all things that I said to you. Peace I leave with you, My peace I give to you; not as the world gives do I give to you. Let not your heart be troubled, neither let it be afraid. You have heard Me say to you, 'I am going away and coming back to you.' If you loved Me, you would rejoice because I said, 'I am going to the Father,' for My Father is greater than I."

Covenants Contain an Exchange of Robes

- Identity

Covenants Contain an Exchange of Weapons

- Armor (see "God's weapons" page 1)

Covenants Contain an Exchange of Enemies

- Protection

Peace: Spiritual Warfare for Blessings

The Priestly Blessing

<u>Numbers 6:22-26</u>

To say, "*shalom,*" in greeting someone, you bless them with all of the definitions of *shalom*.

Peace: Spiritual Warfare for Healing

> **Definition of "peace"**—*shalom*—(Hebrew): "soundness in body and health"

Peace: Rest as Spiritual Warfare

<u>Genesis 2:2-3</u>

Old Testament References Link Peace to Quietness and Rest

<u>Isaiah 32:16-20</u>

<u>Isaiah 57:2:</u>
He shall enter into peace;
They shall rest in their beds,
Each one walking in his uprightness.

> **Definition of "seven":** "complete, all, finished, rest."[16]

"Peace" has two of the same definitions as "seven"—complete and rest.

God Rested on the Seventh Day of Creation

Keeping the Sabbath

Mark 2:27-28:
And He said to them, "The Sabbath was made for man, and not man for the Sabbath. Therefore the Son of Man is also Lord of the Sabbath."

Peace: Spiritual Warfare as Rest for Sleep

Psalm 4:8:
I will both lie down in peace, and sleep;
For You alone, O LORD, make me dwell in safety.

Proverbs 3:24:
When you lie down, you will not be afraid;
Yes, you will lie down and your sleep will be sweet.

Peace: Rest in Warfare

2 Chronicles 14:10-12

2 Chronicles 20:17-30

Rest in the Middle of War

When we are in Christ, we are in covenant with God. His enemies are our enemies, and our enemies are His.

Deuteronomy 32:41:
"If I whet My glittering sword,
And My hand takes hold on judgment,
I will render vengeance to My enemies,
And repay those who hate Me."

What Robs Us of Our Peace in Warfare?

- Belief that God is not going to protect us. Or, the unbelief that God will protect us.

- Belief in the Enemy's lies that we will not be protected.

- Belief that we are not worthy for God to protect us.

Old Testament Connection of Peace and Righteousness

Psalm 85:10

In the Old Testament, we see righteousness brings about Peace. Numbers 25:1-13 gives an example of righteousness bringing about a covenant of Peace.

In contrast, there is no Peace for the wicked.

Isaiah 48:22

Isaiah 32:16-20

New Testament Connection of Peace and Righteousness

Isaiah 9:6:
For unto us a Child is born,
Unto us a Son is given;
And the government will be upon His shoulder.
And His name will be called
Wonderful, Counselor, Mighty God,
Everlasting Father, Prince of Peace.

In the New Testament, Peace is the foundation for righteousness.

Luke 2:14:
"Glory to God in the highest,
And on earth peace, goodwill toward men!"

Peace on Earth

Jesus, God incarnate, as the Prince of Peace is now on earth prophesied in Isaiah 9:6.

> **Definition of "peace"—*shalom*—(Hebrew):** "complete, wholeness and wellbeing"

Hebrews 13:8:
Jesus Christ is the same yesterday, today and forever.

The angels declare blessing on the earth in Luke 2:14. Jesus came to earth to preach the Kingdom of Heaven. Righteousness, Peace and Joy in the Holy Spirit is the Kingdom of God. (Romans 14:17)

James 3:18 shows us that Peace is necessary for a harvest of righteousness.

James 3:18 (ESV):
And a harvest of righteousness is sown in peace by those who make peace.

The angels declare Peace on earth in preparation for Jesus' fruitful ministry of a harvest of righteousness.

God Rules in Peace, and Jesus is the Prince of Peace

Matthew 10:11-15

Peace and Righteousness as Spiritual Warfare

I Thessalonians 5:23-24 (NIV):
May God himself, the God of peace, sanctify you through and through. May your whole spirit, soul and body be kept blameless at the coming of the Lord Jesus Christ. The one who calls you is faithful and he will do it.

It's our God of Peace who sanctifies, which brings about righteousness.

Peace: Spiritual Warfare for Evangelism

Armor: Feet Shod With The Gospel of Peace

Ephesians 6:15 (KJV):
And your feet shod with the preparation of the gospel of peace.

Ephesians 6:15 (AMP):
And having shod your feet in preparation [to face the enemy with the firm-footed stability, the promptness and the readiness produced by the good news] of the Gospel of peace.

The purpose of Peace in the "feet shod with the gospel of Peace" is to prepare a foundation for a harvest of righteousness.

Isaiah 52:7:
How beautiful upon the mountains
Are the feet of him who brings good news,
Who proclaims peace,
Who brings glad tidings of good things,
Who proclaims salvation,
Who says to Zion, "Your God reigns!"

The feet need to be fitted with Peace. It's the Peace that lays the groundwork for righteousness to be in place.

Psalm 119:165:
Great peace have those who love Your law,
And nothing causes them to stumble.

Jesus also shows the correlation between Peace and a harvest of righteousness when He sends out the twelve in the Gospel of Matthew.

Matthew 10:11-15

Ephesians 6:15 commands that the feet be shod with the gospel of Peace. This is different than interpreting it as "feet being shod with Peace."

- ➢ **Definition of "gospel" (Greek):**
  1) "a. *often capitalized*: the message concerning Christ, the kingdom of God, and salvation
     b. *capitalized*: one of the first four New Testament books telling of the life, death, and resurrection of Jesus Christ"[17]

Our covenant of Peace with the Lord includes an exchange of weapons.

James 3:18 (ESV):
And a harvest of righteousness is sown in peace by those who make peace.

Psalm 85:10-13

Peace: Spiritual Warfare Against Satan

Romans 16:20 (NIV):
And the God of peace will soon crush Satan under your feet. The grace of our Lord Jesus be with you.

Significance of the Foot

Placement of the foot on the head or neck of an enemy represents victory.

Part of the armor is the feet shod with the good news of Peace.

Peace: Spiritual Warfare for Those Coming Out of the Occult

Romans 16:20 (NIV):
And the God of peace will soon crush Satan under your feet. The grace of our Lord Jesus be with you.

Isaiah 48:22:
"There is no peace," says the LORD, "for the wicked."

Peace and Kingdom of God: Righteousness, Peace and Joy in the Holy Ghost

Romans 14:17:

When we come out of the kingdom of darkness into the Kingdom of God, we need these components of the Kingdom of God imparted into us: righteousness, Peace and Joy.

Covenant of Peace

Components of Covenant

Exchange of Robes

- Identity

Exchange of Weapons

- Armor

Exchange of Enemies

- Protection

Peace: Spiritual Warfare in Guarding the Heart and Mind

Philippians 4:7:
...and the peace of God, which surpasses all understanding, will guard your hearts and minds through Christ Jesus.

Isaiah 26:3:
"You will keep him in perfect peace,
Whose mind is stayed on You,
Because he trusts in You."

Matthew 11:12:
"And from the days of John the Baptist until now the kingdom of heaven suffers violence, and the violent take it by force."

Notes:

Prayers for Peace

Prayer for Repentance and Impartation of Peace

Dear Heavenly Father, in the name of the Lord Jesus Christ, I recognize I have limited the rule of Your Peace in my life. I repent and ask for Your forgiveness. I change the way I think about Peace. I choose to renew my mind with the truth that I am in a covenant of Peace with You. Peace means "completeness, safety, soundness in body, welfare, health, prosperity, peace, quiet, tranquility, contentment and friendship with You in a covenant relationship; peace in relationships; and peace from war." I repent and ask for Your forgiveness for fear, not resting, unrighteousness and not believing You will heal me. I repent on behalf of all my generations back to Adam and Eve who have not lived in covenant of Peace with You. I bind and break Satan's power and authority over me in the area of stealing Peace in my life and in my generations. I renounce agreement with unrighteousness and undermining of Your reign of Peace in my life.

Heavenly Father, through the power of the Holy Spirit, I give You permission to rule in Peace in my heart. I thank You for Your covenant of Peace that gives me Your identity, Your weapons and Your protection from my enemies. Please teach me through Your Word, through the Holy Spirit, and through intimacy with You how to live in the covenant of Peace You have made with me. Thank You that Peace crushes Satan. Thank You that the covenant of Peace with You includes safety, soundness in body, welfare, health, prosperity, quiet, tranquility, contentment and peace from war. Please bring about justice, restoration and restitution in my life in relation to the Peace that was stolen from me by the Enemy in the areas of rest, evangelism, righteousness, health, finances, prosperity, contentment, safety, and peace from war. In Jesus' name, amen.

Prayer to Break Occult Covenants/Replacement of Covenant of Peace

Dear Heavenly Father, in the name of the Lord Jesus Christ, I recognize I have limited the rule of Your Peace in my life and I repent. I change the way I think about Peace. I choose to renew my mind with the truth that I am in a covenant of Peace with You. Peace means "completeness, safety, soundness in body, welfare, health, prosperity, peace, quiet, tranquility, contentment and friendship with You in a covenant relationship; peace in relationships; and peace from war." I repent ask for forgiveness for the way I and my generations did not live in covenant of Peace with You. I repent and ask for forgiveness of making occult covenants. I come to you as one in a covenant of Peace with Jesus Christ of Nazareth. I renounce all covenants to Satan and the kingdom of darkness. Father, as I am in covenant with Jesus Christ, please annul any of these unholy covenants.

And, with the sword of the Spirit, which is the word of God that is living and powerful, and sharper than any two-edged sword, piercing even to the division of soul and spirit, and of joints and marrow, and is a discerner of the thoughts and intents of the heart-please separate any connections of my spirit, soul and body with anything concerning these occult covenants.

Heavenly Father, through the power of the Holy Spirit, I give You permission to rule in Peace in my heart. I thank You for Your covenant of Peace that gives me Your identity, Your weapons and Your protection from my enemies. Please teach me through Your Word, through the Holy Spirit, and through intimacy with You how to live in the covenant of Peace You have made with me. Thank You that Peace crushes Satan. Thank You that the covenant of Peace with You includes safety, soundness in body, welfare, health, prosperity, quiet, tranquility, contentment and peace from war. Please bring about justice, restoration and restitution in my life in relation to the Peace that was stolen from me by the Enemy in these areas of covenant. In the name of Jesus, amen.

SESSION 6
The Kingdom of God: Righteousness, Peace and Joy

Introduction

Romans 14:16-17:
Therefore do not let your good be spoken of as evil; for the kingdom of God is not eating and drinking, but righteousness and peace and joy in the Holy Spirit.

Connection of Joy and Righteousness

Nehemiah 8:10b:
"...for the joy of the LORD is your strength."

Hebrews 12:1-2

Jesus was filled with Joy to live a righteous life to be the spotless Lamb of God for the ultimate purpose of righteousness—to make us righteous.

Connection of Peace and Righteousness

Psalm 85:10 (NIV):
Love and faithfulness meet together; righteousness and peace kiss each other.

Righteousness, Peace and Joy comprise the Kingdom of God

Genesis 14:18-20

Notes:

The Kingdom of God and the Connection to Peace

> **Definition of "Salem" (Hebrew):** "peace"

- The biblical connection of Salem and Jerusalem

- Jesus' connection to Peace

Isaiah 9:6-7

Revelation 21:1-5

The Kingdom of God and the Connection to Righteousness

Melchizedek Described in More Detail

Hebrews 7:1-2:
For this Melchizedek, king of Salem, priest of the Most High God, who met Abraham returning from the slaughter of the kings and blessed him, to whom also Abraham gave a tenth part of all, first being translated "king of righteousness," and then also king of Salem, meaning "king of peace."

The Kingdom of God Relates to Righteousness and Peace

Melchizedek translates as "king of righteousness," who is the king of Salem, which is the city of Peace. Since he is the king of Salem, he is the "king of peace." This is an example of how righteousness and Peace "kiss each other."

Jesus' Connection to Ruling in Peace and Righteousness

Isaiah 32:1 (KJV):
Behold, a king will reign in righteousness, and princes shall rule in judgment.

- Jesus is the "King of righteousness"

- In Isaiah 9:6, Jesus is named the "Prince of Peace"

- Jesus is described as the "King of kings"

1 Timothy 6:15:
...which He will manifest in His own time, He who is the blessed and only Potentate, the King of kings and Lord of lords...

Revelation 17:14:
"These will make war with the Lamb, and the Lamb will overcome them, for He is Lord of lords and King of kings; and those who are with Him are called, chosen, and faithful."

Revelation 19:16:
And He has on His robe and on His thigh a name written:
　　KING OF KINGS AND LORD OF LORDS.

Notes:

SESSION 7
Patience as Spiritual Warfare

Introduction

Definition of Patience

Galatians 5:22-23 (ESV):
But the fruit of the Spirit is love, joy, peace, patience, kindness, goodness, faithfulness, gentleness, self-control; against such things there is no law.

- **Definition of "patience"—*makrothymia*—(Greek: Strong's 3115):**
    1) "patience, endurance, constancy, steadfastness, perseverance
    2) patience, forbearance, longsuffering, slowness in avenging wrongs"

Romans 15:4-6:
For whatever things were written before were written for our learning, that we through the patience and comfort of the Scriptures might have hope. Now may the God of patience and comfort grant you to be like-minded toward one another, according to Christ Jesus, that you may with one mind and one mouth glorify the God and Father of our Lord Jesus Christ.

- **Definition of "patience"—*hypomonē*—(Greek: Strong's 5281):**
    1) "steadfastness, constancy, endurance
        a) in the New Testament the characteristic of a man who is not swerved from his deliberate purpose and his loyalty to faith and piety by even the greatest trials and sufferings
        b) patiently, and steadfastly
    2) a patient, steadfast waiting for
    3) a patient enduring, sustaining, perseverance"

James 5:8:
You also be patient. Establish your hearts, for the coming of the Lord is at hand.

- **Definition of "patience"—*makrothymeō*—(Greek: Strong's 3114):**
    1) "to be of a long spirit, not to lose heart
        a) to persevere patiently and bravely in enduring misfortunes and troubles
        b) to be patient in bearing the offenses and injuries of others
    2) to be mild and slow in avenging
    3) to be longsuffering, slow to anger, slow to punish"

Patience vs. Self-Control

The application of Self-Control to refrain from acting in anger is not the same as being patient.

Patience: Spiritual Warfare for Unity

Romans 15:1-6

God of Patience and Comfort

- Scripture was written to show the endurance and trustworthiness of the Word of the Lord.

- What does "the Patience of the Scriptures" mean?

- What is the constancy of the Scriptures and the Word of God?

John 1:1-5

Hebrews 13:5:
Let your conduct be without covetousness; be content with such things as you have. For He Himself has said, "I will never leave you nor forsake you."

Jesus is the Word. He is the same yesterday, today and forever (Heb 13:8). We see in Scripture that, as the Word, Jesus is constant and steadfast.

What does the "comfort of the Scriptures" mean?

- **Definition of "comfort"—Romans 15:5—(Greek):** "consolation, comfort, solace; that which affords comfort or refreshment"

Endurance and Comfort are Key for Unity—Romans 15:5

Unity in Scripture

Genesis 11:5-6:
But the LORD came down to see the city and the tower which the sons of men had built. And the LORD said, "Indeed the people are one and they all have one language, and this is what they begin to do; now nothing that they propose to do will be withheld from them."

The Lord said that since the people were united and were one, there was nothing they proposed or purposed to do that could be stopped.

Unity is a powerful weapon of warfare, and Satan knows it.

> **Acts 2:1:**
> *When the Day of Pentecost had fully come, they were all with one accord in one place.*

- ➢ **Definition of "accord" (Greek):** "with one mind, with one accord, with one passion"

We know that on the day of Pentecost, the 120 believers in the upper room that were in "one accord" received the baptism of the Holy Spirit.

> **Acts 2:46-47**

Connection of Jesus and Unity

> **John 17:20-23**

Patience and Unity: Spiritual Warfare for Favor and Redemption

> **Acts 2:46-47:**
> *So continuing daily with one accord in the temple, and breaking bread from house to house, they ate their food with gladness and simplicity of heart, praising God and having favor with all the people. And the Lord added to the church daily those who were being saved.*

- ➢ **Definition of "simplicity" (Greek):** "simplicity and singleness"

Notes:

Steps to Gain Favor in Acts 2:46-47

- They were in one accord.
- They fellowshipped with one another.
- They ate their food in unity of heart.
- They praised the Lord.
- This gladness and Joy led to having favor with all people.

The Greek word here for "people" means: "a people, people group, tribe, nation, all those who are of the same stock and language."

Out of this, the Lord added to the church daily all who were saved. This favor with ALL people brought about a harvest of souls into the Kingdom of God.

The Enemy wants to undermine our unity because he wants to stop the harvest of souls into the Kingdom.

Patience:
Spiritual Warfare as We Wait for Coming of the Lord

James 5:7-11

With patience, Jesus awaits the work to be completed in us while He waits for us to become His bride. He is the farmer in this passage. The precious fruit represents us.

We are to be of a long spirit, not to lose heart; and make stable our soul or mind, as it is the fountain and seat of the thoughts, passions, desires, appetites, affections, purposes and endeavors, for the coming of the Lord is at hand.

Notes:

Patience:
Spiritual Warfare for Endurance

James 1:2-4

Luke 21:7-19

Through endurance and Patience, we will possess our soul.

The Purpose of Patience Is Unity

We need to have Patience with others while we go through our trials to have unity.

James 1:2-4:
My brethren, count it all joy when you fall into various trials, knowing that the testing of your faith produces patience. But let patience have its perfect work, that you may be perfect and complete, lacking nothing.

Notes:

Prayer for Patience

Prayer for Repentance and Impartation of Patience

Dear Heavenly Father, in the name of the Lord Jesus Christ, I recognize I have had a wrong understanding of the purpose of Patience. I repent of applying Self-Control to situations to control my anger instead of being Patient. I repent of not being Patient, which destroys unity. I repent of any times my impatience misrepresented You and destroyed opportunities for You to bring people into the Kingdom because of my behavior. I change the way I think about Patience. Please forgive me, and I forgive myself. I choose to replace my thinking with the truth that Patience is for the purpose of unity and for the salvation of the lost. I bind and break Satan's power and authority over me in the area of focusing on managing my anger and impatience with Self-Control instead of having a change of heart and being Patient. Please forgive my generations back to Adam and Even for undermining the work of unity and bringing in the harvest. I thank You all that Satan's power and authority is broken in the area of not being Patient in all my generations. I renounce agreement with impatience.

Heavenly Father, through the power of the Holy Spirit, please place in me Your Patience for the purpose of unity. Please let me experience You as the God of Patience and comfort. May Your Patience transform me to live in unity with others for Your work to be accomplished on earth as it is in heaven. I desire Your Patience to endure all trials righteously and in unity with You, myself and others. I pray that this Patience and unity would bring many into the Kingdom. I receive Your Patience for the purpose of endurance, unity, and effective evangelism. Please teach me through Your Word, through the Holy Spirit, and through intimacy with You how to live as one who is truly Patient. Thank You that Joy is necessary in trials that through the testing of my Faith produces Patience, and that the perfect work of Patience is that I may be perfect and complete, lacking nothing. Please bring about justice, restoration and restitution in my life concerning the Patience and unity that have been stolen from me by the Enemy. In Jesus' name, amen.

SESSION 8
Kindness as Spiritual Warfare

Kindness: Spiritual Warfare for Repentance

Romans 2:1-4 (NIV):
You, therefore, have no excuse, you who pass judgment on someone else, for at whatever point you judge another, you are condemning yourself, because you who pass judgment do the same things. Now we know that God's judgment against those who do such things is based on truth. So when you, a mere human being, pass judgment on them and yet do the same things, do you think you will escape God's judgment? Or do you show contempt for the riches of his kindness, forbearance and patience, not realizing that God's kindness is intended to lead you to repentance?

Romans 2:4 (AMP):
Or are you [so blind as to] trifle with and presume upon and despise and underestimate the wealth of His kindness and forbearance and long-suffering patience? Are you unmindful or actually ignorant [of the fact] that God's kindness is intended to lead you to repent (to change your mind and inner man to accept God's will)?

The Greek words used for "Kindness" in this verse are two different words "*chrēstotēs*" and "*chrēstos*," respectively; however, both contain the definition of "Kindness" and "Goodness."

Link Between Repentance and Redemption

Repentance leads us to redemption.

Notes:

Kindness:
Spiritual Warfare for Redemption

Law of the Kinsman-Redeemer (Leviticus 25:23-28)

Leviticus 25:25:
"'If one of your brethren becomes poor, and has sold some of his possession, and if his redeeming relative comes to redeem it, then he may redeem what his brother sold.'"

> **Definition of "redeem" (Hebrew):** "redeem, act as kinsman-redeemer, avenge, revenge, ransom, do the part of a kinsman"

Jesus, our Redeemer, sets us free.

John 8:34-36:
Jesus answered them, "Most assuredly, I say to you, whoever commits sin is a slave of sin. And a slave does not abide in the house forever, but a son abides forever. Therefore if the Son makes you free, you shall be free indeed."

The Lord will avenge all who sin against us.

Deuteronomy 32:43:
"Rejoice, O Gentiles, with His people;
For He will avenge the blood of His servants,
And render vengeance to His adversaries;
He will provide atonement for His land and His people."

Through His everlasting Kindness, He will redeem us through His Mercy.

Isaiah 54:8b:
"But with everlasting kindness I will have mercy on you,"
Says the LORD, your Redeemer.

The Levirate Marriage

Deuteronomy 25:5-6:
"If brothers dwell together, and one of them dies and has no son, the widow of the dead man shall not be married to a stranger outside the family; her husband's brother shall go in to her, take her as his wife, and perform the duty of a husband's brother to her. And it shall be that the firstborn son which she bears will succeed to the name of his dead brother, that his name may not be blotted out of Israel."

Kindness in the Book of Ruth

- Naomi uses Kindness first.

- Ruth responds to Boaz' blessing.

Ruth 2:13:
"Then she said, 'Let me find favor in your sight, my lord; for you have comforted me, and have spoken kindly to your maidservant, though I am not like one of your maidservants.'"

- The third time the word "kind" is spoken in Ruth takes place when she returns home from her first day of gleaning.

- Instead of saying, "and have spoken kindly to your maidservant," the Hebrew Interlinear Bible reveals that Ruth's words to Boaz reflect that he spoke on her heart.[18]

Ruth 2:20:
Then Naomi said to her daughter-in-law, "Blessed be he of the LORD, who has not forsaken His kindness to the living and the dead!" And Naomi said to her, "This man is a relation of ours, one of our close relatives."

- Boaz' use of the word Kindness.

Ruth 3:9-13

Boaz is a type of Christ. Ruth's request to him to be her kinsman-redeemer shows Kindness to Boaz. Can it also be said that our response to Jesus to ask Him to redeem us shows Kindness to Jesus?

Kindness:
Connection to Redemption and Mercy

Isaiah 54:8b:
"But with everlasting kindness I will have mercy on you," Says the LORD, your Redeemer.

Through the Lord our redeemer's unending Kindness (*checed*—goodness, kindness, faithfulness), He will have mercy on us. God extends mercy in His Kindness.

> **Definition for "mercy"—*racham*—(Hebrew):** "to love, love deeply, have mercy, be compassionate, have tender affection, have compassion"

"Redeemer" is the same word "*ga'al*" used in Leviticus 25:25 to redeem the land.

Adding the definitions of "kindness," "mercy" and "redeemer" to Isaiah 54:8b, it would say: "But with everlasting kindness (goodness and faithfulness) I will have mercy on you (love you, love you deeply, be compassionate to you, have tender affection to you)," says the LORD your redeemer (the one who is kinsman-redeemer, the one who avenges, the one who takes revenge and the one who ransoms you).

Covenant of Peace

Isaiah 54:10:
"For the mountains shall depart
And the hills be removed,
But My kindness shall not depart from you,
Nor shall My covenant of peace be removed,"
Says the LORD, who has mercy on you.

Kindness:
Spiritual Warfare for Evangelism

Boaz is a type of Christ. Ruth is a type of the Church. It took a special man, Boaz, to see Ruth, a Moabitess from a much-despised gentile nation, for who she was. Boaz' mother, Rahab, was not only a gentile, but a prostitute prior to marrying into what would later be known as the lineage of Jesus. Jesus redeemed us when we were sinners. He knew our value and paid the ransom for our lives. This is good news. As believers, we have entered into the covenant of Peace through Faith made possible by the Kindness and redemption of our Lord. This news of Kindness is what the unredeemed world longs to hear—the Kindness of the Lord has paid the price for redemption.

Kindness:
Spiritual Warfare Against Grieving the Holy Spirit

Kindness opposes evil. It keeps us from grieving the Holy Spirit.

Ephesians 4:29-32:
Let no corrupt word proceed out of your mouth, but what is good for necessary edification, that it may impart grace to the hearers. And do not grieve the Holy Spirit of God, by whom you were sealed for the day of redemption. Let all bitterness, wrath, anger, clamor, and evil speaking be put away from you, with all malice. And be kind to one another, tenderhearted, forgiving one another, even as God in Christ forgave you.

Kindness:
Spiritual Warfare Against Judgment and for Repentance—Initial Repentance and Continual Repentance

Kindness is relevant in our lives for repentance as believers, as well as for those who are not yet believers.

Romans 2:1-4 (AMP):
Therefore you have no excuse or defense or justification, O man, whoever you are who judges and condemns another. For in posing as judge and passing sentence on another, you condemn yourself, because you who judge are habitually practicing the very same things [that you censure and denounce].

[But] we know that the judgment (adverse verdict, sentence) of God falls justly and in accordance with truth upon those who practice such things.

And do you think or imagine, O man, when you judge and condemn those who practice such things and yet do them yourself, that you will escape God's judgment and elude His sentence and adverse verdict?

Or are you [so blind as to] trifle with and presume upon and despise and underestimate the wealth of His kindness and forbearance and long-suffering patience? Are you unmindful or actually ignorant [of the fact] that God's kindness is intended to lead you to repent (to change your mind and inner man to accept God's will)?

The book of Romans speaks of not judging others because we will be judged the way we judge. We do what we judge others for. We must come in Kindness, the opposite spirit of judgment, to bring people into the Kingdom through repentance. Kindness, for believers, leads to repentance from sin in our daily lives.

God's Kindness gives us safety to see things in our lives we need to give to Him and to repent from.

Likewise, we can extend this Kindness to others in the Body of Christ. This creates a safe place to walk in greater intimacy with the Father so others can lay aside the strongholds that vie for the place of the Father in their hearts.

We can create an atmosphere of spiritual safety for those around us to grow in the area of righteousness.

Notes:

Prayer for Kindness

Kindness: Repentance Prayer and Prayer for Impartation

Dear Heavenly Father, in the name of the Lord Jesus Christ, I recognize I have sinned in rejecting and despising Your Kindness toward me and toward others. I haven't understood the Kindness You have for me and have rejected it. I have been judgmental toward myself and others instead of being kind. Also, I have not understood the connection of Your Love and Mercy, which are fully mine because of Your Kindness. (Add anything else here the Holy Spirit leads you to repent of.) I repent of these sins. Forgive me for any ways that I have not been kind and by being judgmental of others or myself, for not accepting Your Kindness for myself, and for not representing Your Kindness to others. Father, please forgive all my generations back to Adam and Eve for all ways that we have not been kind. I bind and break all of Satan's power and authority over my life and all my generations in this area. Please restore to me all that has been lost and stolen from me in my life and my generations in regard to Kindness. Please expand my area of influence in the lives of people through Kindness.

Dear Heavenly Father, please teach me through the Holy Spirit more about Your Kindness. I receive Your Kindness. Please speak on my heart with Your Kindness. Not only do I desire to have You speak on my heart, I also desire to speak on the hearts of others. Thank You for the love story of Boaz and Ruth to demonstrate once again the Love of Your Son Jesus Christ for me. Please impart Your Kindness to me so that I may be effective in Your Kingdom to bring others into relationship with You. Your Kindness leads to repentance, not only in my life to transform me from glory to glory, but also in the lives of others so that they may be transformed from glory to glory. May I truly reflect Your nature of Kindness that I may be helpful and useful in the lives of those whom You have placed in my sphere of influence. In Jesus' name, amen.

SESSION 9
Goodness as Spiritual Warfare

Introduction

Romans 12:21:
Do not be overcome by evil, but overcome evil with good.

Psalm 27:13:
*I would have lost heart, unless I had believed
That I would see the goodness of the LORD
In the land of the living.*

Definition of Goodness in Scripture

Micah 6:8:
*He has shown you, O man, what is good;
And what does the LORD require of you
But to do justly,
To love mercy,
And to walk humbly with your God?*

Isaiah 1:16-17:
*"Wash yourselves, make yourselves clean;
Put away the evil of your doings from before My eyes.
Cease to do evil,
Learn to do good;
Seek justice, rebuke the oppressor;
Defend the fatherless,
Plead for the widow."*

Notes:

Goodness:
Justice as Spiritual Warfare

Micah 6:8:
*He has shown you, O man, **what is good**;*
And what does the LORD require of you
*But **to do justly**,*
To love mercy,
And to walk humbly with your God? (Emphasis added.)

Isaiah 1:16-17 is specific when it says, "learn to do good."

Isaiah 1:16-17:
"Seek justice,
Rebuke the oppressor,
Defend the fatherless,
Plead for the widow."

Goodness and Justice

What do justice, rebuking the oppressor, defending the fatherless and pleading for the widow all have in common? Father God carries out all of these responsibilities.

How does justice being carried out show us the Goodness of the nature of God and how does it fit into His functions in the Godhead? The nature of God is Good; therefore, He is Good in protection, provision and giving identity. Justice encompasses all three of these functions.

Deuteronomy 32:35:
"Vengeance is Mine, and recompense...."

Deuteronomy 32:43:
"Rejoice, O Gentiles, with His people;
For He will avenge the blood of His servants,
And render vengeance to His adversaries;
He will provide atonement for His land and His people."

Nahum 1:2-3:
God is jealous, and the LORD avenges;
The LORD avenges and is furious.
The LORD will take vengeance on His adversaries,
And He reserves wrath for His enemies;
The LORD is slow to anger and great in power,
And will not at all acquit the wicked.

Justice Involves Restoration and Restitution

Restoration brings us back to our former position or condition. Justice includes restitution.

In the Kingdom of God, He returns things back to His original design for a person's life, not necessarily the original condition the person was in beforehand.

Joseph is a Biblical Example of Justice, Restoration and Restitution

<u>Genesis 37</u>

<u>Proverbs 6:30-31</u>:
People do not despise a thief
If he steals to satisfy himself when he is starving.
Yet when he is found, he must restore sevenfold;
He may have to give up all the substance of his house.

Restitution is one aspect of how the Father brings about provision and exacts justice on our behalf. He can provide for us by restoring to us with increase what the Enemy stole from us.

Justice Gives Identity, Protection and Provision

<u>Isaiah 1:16-17</u>

Widows and orphans are recipients of identity, protection and provision when justice is exacted on their behalf.

Notes:

Goodness:
Mercy as Spiritual Warfare

Micah 6:8:
*He has shown you, O man, **what is good**;*
And what does the LORD require of you
But to do justly,
To love mercy,
And to walk humbly with your God? (Emphasis added.)

Psalm 23:6:
Surely goodness and mercy shall follow me
All the days of my life;
And I will dwell in the house of the LORD forever.

Goodness and Mercy are intimately connected throughout Scripture.

Mercy Triumphs Over Judgment

Psalm 25:7:
Do not remember the sins of my youth, nor my transgressions;
According to Your mercy remember me,
For Your goodness' sake, O LORD.

James 2:12-13:
So speak and so do as those who will be judged by the law of liberty. For judgment is without mercy to the one who has shown no mercy. Mercy triumphs over judgment.

Detailed teaching on this is in Session 10. This is a placeholder to show the logical progression of how Goodness transitions to Justice and then to Mercy.

Goodness and Mercy:
Spiritual Warfare Against Judgment and Guilt

James 2:13:
Mercy triumphs over judgment.

Detailed teaching on this is in Session 10. This is a placeholder to show the logical progression of how Goodness transitions to Justice and then to Mercy.

Goodness:
Humility as Spiritual Warfare

Micah 6:8:
*He has shown you, O man, **what is good**;*
And what does the LORD *require of you*
But to do justly,
To love mercy,
And to walk humbly with your God? *(Emphasis added.)*

Humility keeps us in the proper perspective of who God is. It keeps us in the proper respect of who we are in relation to Him.

Goodness and Glory:
Spiritual Warfare Over the Spirit of Leviathan (Pride)

Detailed teaching on this is in Session 11. This is a placeholder to show the logical progression of how Goodness transitions to Mercy and then to Humility.

God's Glory Is His Goodness

Exodus 33:18-23:
And he [Moses] said, "Please, show me Your glory."

Then He said, "I will make all My goodness pass before you, and I will proclaim the name of the LORD *before you…."*

➢ **Definition of "glory" (Hebrew):** "weight, splendor, abundance"

Glory refers to all God is and does.

Goodness:
Glory as Spiritual Warfare

Isaiah 58:8:
Then your light shall break forth like the morning,
Your healing shall spring forth speedily,
And your righteousness shall go before you;
The glory of the LORD *shall be your rear guard.*

Isaiah 52:12:
For you shall not go out with haste,
Nor go by flight;
For the LORD will go before you,
And the God of Israel will be your rear guard.

Psalm 24:7-10:
Lift up your heads, O you gates!
And be lifted up, you everlasting doors!
And the King of glory shall come in.

Who is this King of glory?
The LORD strong and mighty,
The LORD mighty in battle.

Lift up your heads, O you gates!
Lift up, you everlasting doors!
And the King of glory shall come in.

Who is this King of glory?
The LORD of hosts,
He is the King of glory.

> **Definition of "rear guard"—*'acaph*—(Hebrew):** "to gather" and "to bring up the rear"

We have a mighty God who covers our back. Because of this, we need not be hasty when it comes to warfare.

We are not at the Enemy's beck and call. The word "beck" comes from the word beckon, which means, "to summon or signal typically with a wave or a nod."[19] We are not to rush into engagement with the Enemy because he looks at us or calls out to us. Just as the Israelites sought God in the Old Testament about whether or not to go into battle, we need to do the same. The Lord will let us know when the battle will be strategic. He will also help us to stay out of or avoid battles that the Enemy wants to engage us in for the purpose of wearing us down.

One of the components of our rear guard is glory.

Glory is God's Goodness. The glory of the Lord is His splendor, abundance and majesty. His Goodness contains Justice, Mercy and Humility.

The Goodness of God Satisfies as Spiritual Warfare

Jeremiah 31:14:
*"I will satiate the soul of the priests with abundance,
And My people shall be satisfied with My goodness, says the LORD."*

Psalm 65:4:
*Blessed is the man You choose,
And cause to approach You,
That he may dwell in Your courts.
We shall be satisfied with the goodness of Your house,
Of Your holy temple.*

- **Definition of "satisfied"—*saba`*—(Hebrew):** "to be fulfilled, be sated, be surfeited"

- **Definition of "sated" (Webster):** "to cloy with overabundance" and is commonly used in reference to food"[20]

- **Definition of "surfeited" (Webster):** "an overabundant supply"[21]

- **Definition of "satisfied" (Webster):** is used in the context of a contract being carried out in full and the meeting of a financial obligation[22]

What Does Satan Use to Attack God's Goodness?

The Enemy uses all evil is an attack on God's Goodness. Evil is unbelief in God and the truth of everything He says. Evil attacks His nature of Goodness.

- Bitterness sells us the lie that God isn't good enough to care for and protect us.

- Unforgiveness offers a false sense of protection.

- Jealousy and envy are rooted in bitterness.

- Self-hatred undermines the immense value and worth given to us by God. It prevents us from receiving His good gifts.

- The Spirit of Poverty acts as a roadblock to experiencing the abundance of God. It deprives us of the resources that belong to us in Christ.

- The Orphan Spirit opposes our true identity as sons and daughters. It blinds us to the authority that is ours in Christ.

- When we live in the fullness of the Goodness of God, we live in abundance. All areas of lack are obliterated.

Notes:

Prayers for Goodness

Goodness: Repentance Prayer and Prayer of Impartation

Dear Heavenly Father, please forgive me for any way I have sinned according to Goodness in the following:
- for overlooking or not giving much notice to Your Goodness;
- for I have misrepresenting Your Goodness to those You have placed in my life;
- for not being just;
- for not loving mercy;
- for not walking humbly with You;
- for not seeking justice;
- for not rebuking the oppressor;
- for not defending the fatherless;
- for not pleading for the widow;
- for not being satisfied with Your Goodness;
- for using evil as an attempt to overcome evil instead of using Good to overcome evil;
- and for overlooking or underestimating Your glory and Your Goodness.

I receive Your forgiveness and I forgive myself. I also repent and ask for forgiveness for any way my generations participated in and agreed with these things. I break all of Satan's power and authority in my life and in all my generations back to Adam and Eve. Father, please show me Your Goodness. Let me see Your Goodness in the land of the living. I want to taste and see that You are Good. I praise You and give You thanks for Your Goodness and Your Mercy that endure forever. Please transform my heart and my life with Your abundant Goodness. In Jesus' name, amen.

Prayer for Justice, Restoration and Restitution

Dear Heavenly Father, in the name of the Lord Jesus Christ, I come to You and ask for justice regarding the loss of (name the items that has been stolen, killed and/or destroyed from You or Your generations by the Enemy). I repent of all the ways that I or my generations gave legal grounds for this by (for example, being fearful, lying, stealing, etc.). Please forgive me and all my generations. I forgive myself and my generations. I bind and break all of Satan's power and authority over me and my generations in these areas. You are my Judge. I ask You for justice. I ask You for sevenfold restoration and restitution of all that has been stolen, killed or destroyed (list items that the Enemy has stolen, killed and/or destroyed in your life and your generations.) in my life and in my generations. Please heal the wound in my soul that was caused by my loss so that I may be whole and a good steward of all that You will restore to me. I forgive the person who committed this sin against me. I release him or her from any debt owed to me. I choose to relinquish this and allow You to make it right. I thank You for Jesus coming to bring abundant life. I receive the abundance of Your Goodness, Justice and Mercy in my life. In Jesus' name, amen.

SESSION 10
Goodness and Mercy—Spiritual Warfare Against Judgment and Guilt

What Is Guilt?

Guilt is a legal outcome of a judgment.

What Is Judgment?

Luke 6:35-38:
"But if you love those who love you, what credit is that to you? For even sinners love those who love them. And if you do good to those who do good to you, what credit is that to you? For even sinners do the same. And if you lend to those from whom you hope to receive back, what credit is that to you? For even sinners lend to sinners to receive as much back. But love your enemies, do good, and lend, hoping for nothing in return; and your reward will be great, and you will be sons of the Most High. For He is kind to the unthankful and evil. Therefore be merciful, just as your Father also is merciful.

"Judge not, and you shall not be judged. Condemn not, and you shall not be condemned. Forgive, and you will be forgiven. Give, and it will be given to you: good measure, pressed down, shaken together, and running over will be put into your bosom. For with the same measure that you use, it will be measured back to you."

Matthew 6:14-15:
"For if you forgive men their trespasses, your heavenly Father will also forgive you. But if you do not forgive men their trespasses, neither will your Father forgive your trespasses."

Matthew 7:1-5

Notes:

Judgment vs. Discernment

Discernment

Matthew 7:15-20:
"Beware of false prophets, who come to you in sheep's clothing, but inwardly they are ravenous wolves. You will know them by their fruits. Do men gather grapes from thornbushes or figs from thistles? Even so, every good tree bears good fruit, but a bad tree bears bad fruit. A good tree cannot bear bad fruit, nor can a bad tree bear good fruit. Every tree that does not bear good fruit is cut down and thrown into the fire. Therefore by their fruits you will know them."

Judgment

Notes:

Mercy Triumphs Over Judgment

James 2:12-13:
So speak and so do as those who will be judged by the law of liberty. For judgment is without mercy to the one who has shown no mercy. Mercy triumphs over judgment.

- **Definition of "mercy"—*eleos*—(Greek):** "mercy, of God towards men: in general providence; the mercy and clemency of God in providing and offering to men salvation by Christ."

Psalm 116:5:
Gracious is the LORD, and righteous;
Yes, our God is merciful.

- **Definition of "mercy"—*racham*—(Hebrew):** "to love, love deeply, have mercy, be compassionate, have tender affection, have compassion."

Mercy Is Found in God's Goodness

Psalm 23:6:
Surely goodness and mercy shall follow me
All the days of my life;
And I will dwell in the house of the LORD
Forever.

Psalm 25:7:
Do not remember the sins of my youth, nor my transgressions;
According to Your mercy remember me,
For Your goodness' sake, O LORD.

Micah 6:8:
He has shown you, O man, what is good;
And what does the LORD require of you
But to do justly,
To love mercy,
And to walk humbly with your God?

- **Definition of "mercy"**—*hesed*—**(Hebrew):** It is translated in other passages as "lovingkindness."

Guilt Producers

- Not being merciful

- Being judgmental or critical

- Perfectionism
    - Never able to measure up to their own standards of perfection
    - Judgment of self that flows to others
    - Is not rooted in mercy, which leads being judgmental

- Jealousy and Envy
    - Critical and judgmental

- Prophet and prophetic redemptive gift[23]
    - Different than having a spiritual gift of prophecy
    - Has a strong tendency to have little to no mercy
    - Sees things as black and white, right and wrong

69

- Religious Spirit
    - Definition: "seeks religious activity as a substitution for the power of the Holy Spirit"[24]
    - Critical
    - Judgmental
    - Perfectionism

- Legalistic Spirit
    - Definition: "strict concerning the law"
    - Has no mercy for transgressions
    - Judgmental

- Unloving and Self-hatred
    - Perfectionism
    - Religious Spirit
    - Self-condemnation and self-judgment

- Jezebel Spirit
    - Critical
    - Judgmental
    - Religious Spirit
    - No mercy

- Being a recipient of previous nine items from:
    - Family
    - Organizations and denominations
    - Friends
    - Boss
    - Coworkers
    - Others

Freedom from Guilt

Repent of any of these guilt producers and anything else the Holy Spirit may reveal.

1. Recognize
2. Responsibility
3. Repent
4. Renounce
5. Remove
6. Replace

Repent of unforgiveness, fear, etc. pertaining to being the recipient of the items listed above or anything else the Holy Spirit may reveal.

Go through the six steps listed above, beginning with "recognize" and ending with "replace."

Replace judgment and criticism with God's Goodness and Mercy.

Pray for God's justice for the mercy that was stolen through being judgmental or having been judged. Ask for His restoration and restitution for the times mercy was replaced with judgment.

Notes:

Prayers for Goodness and Mercy

Prayer to Repent for Judging Self and Others (Freedom from Guilt)

Dear Heavenly Father, in the name of the Lord Jesus Christ, I recognize I have sinned by judging others and not being merciful. I take responsibility for this and ask You to forgive me for judging (name the person you have judged—you may also want to include yourself). I change the way I think about this sin. I ask You to forgive me. I forgive myself.

I recognize I have sinned and need to repent of any ways I have acted with a Jezebel Spirit, Religious Spirit, Legalistic Spirit, perfectionism and by misusing the gift of discerning of spirits in judgment, criticism and unforgiveness. I take responsibility for these sins and I repent. Please forgive me. I forgive myself. Please forgive all my generations for acting in agreement in these areas of judging others and not allowing You to be the righteous Judge. I bind and break all of Satan's power and authority over me and all my generations regarding these sins. I break all judgment held against me and my generations due to our sins of judging, criticism and not forgiving. I break all the guilt that is associated with the judgment, criticism and unforgiveness. I renounce all agreement with the judgment I have participated in. I relinquish the role of judge and allow You to be the righteous Judge. I declare that I am righteous by the blood of Jesus. I recognize there is a difference between judgment and discernment. I declare all of Satan's power and authority over me and in all my generations is broken. It's by the blood of Jesus and His forgiveness that I am released from all judgment and the verdict of "guilty." Please minister to me through the power of the Holy Spirit and tell me Your truth. In Jesus' name, amen.

Prayer to Forgive Others for Judgment Toward You (Freedom from Guilt)

Dear Heavenly Father, in the name of the Lord Jesus Christ, I recognize I have sinned by holding on to unforgiveness toward those who have judged me (name the person—it could be someone with a Jezebel Spirit, a Religious Spirit, a Legalistic Spirit, or a perfectionist or someone who has judged you in passing). I take responsibility for the unforgiveness and I repent. I ask You to forgive me for my unforgiveness toward this person and any judgment I passed on in my hurt and in retaliation. I forgive myself for holding unforgiveness toward those who judged me. I forgive all who have judged me, whether I am aware of their judgment or not. I release these people from any and all debt owed to me in these situations. I bless them in the name of Jesus. I break any and all curses placed on me through the judgment of others. I also forgive all who have placed judgment on all my generations back to Adam and Eve. I break all of Satan's power and authority over me and in all my generations that was a result of receiving and coming into agreement with the judgment of others. I break all guilt that was a result of the judgment. I am righteous by the blood of Jesus. I declare I am released from all judgment and the verdict of "guilty" from others. Please minister to me through the power of the Holy Spirit and tell me Your truth. In Jesus' name, amen.

Prayer for Impartation of Mercy

Heavenly Father, please forgive me for any ways I have despised Your Mercy, and for any ways I have not trusted You to be Faithful to be a fair, righteous, merciful Judge who vindicates His children. I change the way I think about these sins. Thank you for your forgiveness. I forgive myself. I ask for You to please forgive all my generations for any times Mercy was not given or was hated and for not trusting You to be the righteous Judge. I bind and break all of Satan's power in my life and my generations associated with not being merciful, and for not trusting You to be a good and merciful Judge. It is Your command that we are to be merciful as You are merciful. Please give me a heart of Mercy. May I understand and receive Your Mercy for me so I can demonstrate a life of Mercy to those in my sphere of influence. You are my Judge, I ask You for justice, restoration and restitution for the ways the Enemy has stolen Mercy from me and my generations by the inability to extend mercy, as well as the times mercy was denied to us by others. Please minister to me through the power of the Holy Spirit and tell me Your truth. In Jesus' name, amen.

SESSION 11
Goodness and Glory as Spiritual Warfare Against the Spirit of Leviathan

Introduction

- The characteristics of Leviathan as described in Job 41.

- God's Goodness and glory are effective weapons over Leviathan.

Leviathan

> **Definition of Leviathan (Hebrew):**
> 1) "leviathan, sea monster, dragon;
>   a) large aquatic animal
>   b) perhaps the extinct dinosaur, plesiosaurus, exact definition unknown"

Leviathan is a physical being as well as a spiritual being. It is described in appearance as a "sea monster." From the spiritual aspect, Leviathan is referred to as "the crooked serpent; He will slay the dragon that is in the sea." The Book of Revelation references a dragon, defining him as "Satan" and "the Devil."

References of Leviathan as a Natural and Physical Being

Job 41:1 (KJV):
Canst thou draw out leviathan with an hook? or his tongue with a cord which thou lettest down?

Psalm 104:26 (KJV):
There go the ships: there is that leviathan, whom thou hast made to play therein.

References of Leviathan as a Spiritual Being

"Leviathan" refers to a spiritual being as "a serpent," "dragon," "the Devil" and "Satan."

Isaiah 27:1 (KJV):
In that day the LORD with his sore and great and strong sword shall punish leviathan the piercing serpent, even leviathan that crooked serpent; and he shall slay the dragon that is in the sea.

Revelation 20:1-3a (NKJV):
Then I saw an angel coming down from heaven, having the key to the bottomless pit and a great chain in his hand. He laid hold of the dragon, that serpent of old, who is the Devil and Satan, and bound him for a thousand years; and he cast him into the bottomless pit, and shut him up, and set a seal on him, so that he should deceive the nations no more till the thousand years were finished.

Scripture Linking Physical and Spiritual Aspects of Leviathan

In Job 41, God speaks of the physical attributes of Leviathan and the spiritual characteristics of Satan.

Job 41:34 (KJV):
He beholdeth all high things: he is a king over all the children of pride.

- Lucifer was cast out of heaven because of the sins he committed in his pride.

- Children of pride represent those who walk in pride, as well as generational pride.

- Other aspects that are part of Leviathan and pride mentioned in Job 41 include: gossip; slander; lies; accusations; empty talk; idle talk; anger; distortion of discernment of spirits that leads to judgment, criticism and condemnation; without mercy, which brings in judgment, criticism and condemnation; has no Gentleness, which means anger is present and greatness, inheritance, humility and meekness are undermined; stubbornness; devourer; pride; haughtiness; boasting to make a fool; to make into a fool; to act madly; act like a madman; loftiness; self-exaltation; to instill fear into the mighty and strong as it steals one's destiny and strength; promising power and control; and deception.

Job 41

vs. 1 *"Can you draw out Leviathan with a hook,
Or snare his tongue with a line which you lower?"*

- Leviathan uses his tongue to gossip, slander, lie, accuse.

- Satan is the accuser of the brethren, the father of lies.

vs. 2 *"Can you put a reed through his nose,
Or pierce his jaw with a hook?"*

> **Definition of "nose" (Hebrew):** "nostril and anger"

SESSION 11: GOODNESS AND GLORY

- Prophetically, "nose" is symbolic of discernment because the nose is used to smell. It is able to distinguish among different scents. Things we smell can bring us Joy, such as the scent of our favorite flower, or can alert us to danger, such as the smell of smoke.

- If the nose represents discernment and can be translated here as "discernment," we can put them both together and see that anger twists discerning of spirits. It changes something good into judgment, criticism and condemnation. When we refuse to come into agreement with judgment, we become effective in discerning the spirits that are at work and are able to wage necessary warfare to bless the work of the Holy Spirit, allowing us to liberally promote the work of the Cross.

vs. 3 *"Will he make many supplications to you?*
Will he speak softly to you?"

> **Definition of "supplications" (Hebrew):** "favor"

- Will Leviathan ask for mercy?

- In the face of mercy, Leviathan will not be gentle. Thus, he seeks to undermine the greatness, inheritance, meekness and humility that belong to us through Gentleness in the Lord.

vs. 4 *"Will he make a covenant with you?*
Will you take him as a servant forever?"

- Leviathan seeks to make a covenant and lies about it. He promises he will be our servant and that through this covenant we can have power and control.

vs. 5 *"Will you play with him as with a bird,*
Or will you leash him for your maidens?"

- Leviathan cannot be a pet. Wild animals are not safe pets. At any moment, no matter how well-trained, they can turn and attack. How many times do we think anger, gossip and pride in small amounts can be "pet" sins we can keep under control? On the contrary, these are much bigger than we can control. They end up controlling us.

vs. 6 *"Will your companions make a banquet of him?*
Will they apportion him among the merchants?

vs. 7 *Can you fill his skin with harpoons,*
Or his head with fishing spears?

vs. 8 *Lay your hand on him;*
Remember the battle—
Never do it again!"

- In the spiritual sense, how many times have we tried to battle the Spirit of Leviathan in an attempt to overcome anger, gossip, slander, pride, etc. by the power of our own strength, self-control, sheer will and determination, only to be overtaken by him? We are well-intentioned in our desire to overcome him, but we are not effective. This passage shows that physical weapons of warfare are not effective.

vs. 9 *"Indeed, any hope of overcoming him is false;*
Shall one not be overwhelmed at the sight of him?

vs. 10 *No one is so fierce that he would dare stir him up.*
Who then is able to stand against Me?"

- The Lord will fight Leviathan for us.

vs. 11 *"Who has preceded Me, that I should pay him?*
Everything under heaven is Mine."

vs. 12 *"I will not conceal his limbs,*
His mighty power, or his graceful proportions."

  ➢ **Definition of "conceal" (Hebrew):** "to be silent"

  ➢ **Definition of "limbs" (Hebrew):** "empty talk, idle talk, liar, lie"

- The Lord will not be silent about Leviathan's empty talk, idle talk, lies or the fact that he is a liar. Satan is the father of lies.

John 8:42-44

vs. 13 *"Who can remove his outer coat?*
Who can approach him with a double bridle?"

- Double bridles are used in the tradition of fighting on horseback. Warriors need to be well-trained in the use of a double bridle. They need to be gentle and knowledgeable about its use so as not to hurt the horse. In addition, the horse requires training. A horse that is just starting its training could be injured if the double bridle were applied too soon.

- The purpose of the double bridle is for seven points of control:

    1. Tongue
    2. Bars of the mouth (the gums where there are no teeth)
    3. Lips (corners of the mouth)
    4. Roof of the mouth
    5. Indirectly, the nose
    6. Curb groove (under the chin)
    7. Poll (immediately behind the ears)[25]

- Here, the Lord asks if a trained warrior can bridle Leviathan in warfare. The answer is that none can tame the tongue of pride. We cannot approach pride with the mindset that we can tame it.

  James 3:8:
  But no man can tame the tongue. It is an unruly evil, full of deadly poison.

  Luke 6:45:
  A good man out of the good treasure of his heart brings forth good; and an evil man out of the evil treasure of his heart brings forth evil. For out of the abundance of the heart his mouth speaks.

- We are not to tame the tongue. It is not possible. But, we are to be victorious over it. We need the work of God's Goodness to change our heart that produces Good treasures in it. Only when there is Goodness in us can we speak out Goodness.

vs. 14 *"Who can open the doors of his face,*
With his terrible teeth all around?"

- Mouths are used to eat.

➤ **Definition of "eat" (Webster's 1828):** "to consume and oppress, as in Psalm 14:4, 'Who eat up my people as they eat bread.'"[26]

- This exemplifies what Leviathan does with his mouth—he devours.

vs. 15 *"His rows of scales are his pride,*
Shut up tightly as with a seal;

vs. 16 *One is so near another*
That no air can come between them;

vs. 17 *They are joined one to another,*
They stick together and cannot be parted."

- Leviathan's armor is his pride and nothing penetrates it.

vs. 18 *"His sneezings flash forth light,*
And his eyes are like the eyelids of the morning."

➤ **Definition of "flash" (Hebrew):** "to be boastful; to make a fool of, make into a fool; to act madly, act like a madman"

- Pride is boastful—it seeks to make fools of others but actually makes the prideful one a fool. Acting madly makes one act like a madman—crazy.

vs. 19 *"Out of his mouth go burning lights;*
Sparks of fire shoot out.

vs. 20 *Smoke goes out of his nostrils,*
As from a boiling pot and burning rushes.

vs. 21 *His breath kindles coals,*
And a flame goes out of his mouth."

> **Definition of "breath" (Hebrew):** "soul, self, life, creature, person, appetite, mind, living being, desire, emotion, passion"

- Leviathan's soul kindles the fire of anger and pride.

> **Definition of "flame" (Hebrew):** "flame or blade"

- A blade goes out of the mouth of Leviathan. From the context of this Scripture, blade is anger, lies, empty talk, idle talk, etc. Out of Leviathan's soul comes the destruction of the blade of his anger, lies and idle talk.

vs. 22 *"Strength dwells in his neck,*
And sorrow dances before him."

- Neck represents stubbornness. The phrase "stiff-necked" refers to stubbornness.

- Leviathan takes pleasure in sorrow.

vs. 23 *"The folds of his flesh are joined together;*
They are firm on him and cannot be moved.

vs. 24 *His heart is as hard as stone,*
Even as hard as the lower millstone."

- Leviathan is hard-hearted.

- A new heart can only come from the Lord.

Ezekiel 36:26:
"I will give you a new heart and put a new spirit within you; I will take the heart of stone out of your flesh and give you a heart of flesh."

vs. 25 *"When he raises himself up, the mighty are afraid;*
Because of his crashings they are beside themselves."

- Leviathan uses fear to take away the strength of the mighty. This fear serves to undermine our mighty destiny, purpose and victory. If we battle with fear, we know from this Scripture we are under attack of an evil spirit. The purpose of the attack stems from the fact we are made mighty in God. We can have assurance even in the face of fear.

vs. 26 *"Though the sword reaches him, it cannot avail;*
Nor does spear, dart, or javelin.

vs. 27 *He regards iron as straw,*
And bronze as rotten wood.

vs. 28 *The arrow cannot make him flee;*
Slingstones become like stubble to him.

vs. 29 *Darts are regarded as straw;*
He laughs at the threat of javelins.

vs. 30 *His undersides are like sharp potsherds;*
He spreads pointed marks in the mire.

vs. 31 *He makes the deep boil like a pot;*
He makes the sea like a pot of ointment.

vs. 32 *He leaves a shining wake behind him;*
One would think the deep had white hair.

vs. 33 *On earth there is nothing like him,*
Which is made without fear."

- Leviathan disregards and laughs at anything we use against him that is natural in origin. There is one thing he will not laugh at—God in the fullness of His Goodness and glory.

vs. 34 *"He beholds every high thing;*
He is king over all the children of pride."

- Leviathan, also known as Satan, is king over all the children of pride. A child of pride is one who is a follower of or participator in pride. In the begotten sense of children of pride, it can relate to pride in our past generations. Jesus is our King of kings. In Him, there is no pride. We are transformed from glory to glory.

Glory and Goodness: Spiritual Warfare Against Leviathan

- **Definition of "good" (Micah 6:8):** "to do justly, to love mercy and to walk humbly with your God"

Glory as Spiritual Warfare

Isaiah 58:6-8

Goodness and Glory in Relationship to the Armor of God

What about the armor of God as weapons against Leviathan? In Job, weapons are powerless against him.

The key to the armor is to be in relationship with the One who is Good. We need to know how Goodness and glory are part of the armor of God.

His armor contains the belt of truth, breastplate of righteousness, shield of Faith, feet fitted with the gospel of Peace, the helmet of salvation, the sword of the Spirit, which is the Word of God.

Connecting Goodness, Glory and the Fruit of the Holy Spirit as Spiritual Warfare Against Leviathan

God's Goodness and glory as warfare over Leviathan cannot be looked at in a vacuum.

God is Love. His Goodness is based in Love and is evident in all of the Fruit of the Holy Spirit.

Notes:

God Is the One Who Will Defeat Leviathan

Through His Goodness and glory, we can have victory over Leviathan.

We need to repent of pride, self-exaltation, anger, accusations, lies, idle talk, slander, judgment, criticism and condemnation in our lives and in our generations. We need to ask God to put a heart of flesh in us.

We need His Goodness and glory to fight this battle for us.

We need His Goodness to live justly, to love Mercy and to be Humble in our walk with Him.

Prayer for Goodness and Glory

Prayer for Repentance of Spirit of Leviathan and Impartation of Goodness and Glory

Dear Heavenly Father, in the name of the Lord Jesus Christ, I recognize I have sinned by agreeing with the Spirit of Leviathan. I take responsibility for my pride and repent. I choose to change the way I think about pride and all of its manifestations and replace it with Your Goodness and glory. Please forgive me for any times I have done the following:
- for gossiping;
- for slandering;
- for lying;
- for accusing myself or others;
- for speaking with empty talk;
- for speaking idle talk;
- for having anger toward myself or others;
- for having anger that distorted discerning of spirits which led to judgment, criticism and condemnation;
- for not having mercy, which brings in judgment, criticism and condemnation;
- for not having Gentleness, which means anger is present allowing it to undermine greatness in me and my ability to impart greatness to others;
- for not having Gentleness, which undermines my inheritance, humility and meekness;
- for being stubborn;
- for using my mouth to devour people;
- for being prideful;
- for being haughty;
- for boasting to make a fool of someone;
- for boasting that made me into a fool;
- for acting madly and acted like a madman;
- for acting in loftiness;
- for acting with self-exaltation;
- for allowing the Enemy to instill fear into me;
- for instilling fear into others to break down the mighty and strong which undermines their destiny in You;
- for believing Satan's promises to give power and control;
- and for being deceived and for deceiving others.

Please forgive me and my generations for any ways we have participated in agreement with the Spirit of Leviathan. I receive Your forgiveness and I forgive myself and my generations. Please remove my heart of stone and place within me a heart of flesh. I give to You all my participation with the Spirit of Leviathan and ask that You replace it with Your Goodness and glory. I accept Your weapons of warfare. I renounce the weapons of warfare that are used by the Spirit of Leviathan.

Please release Your Goodness and glory in my life for victory over Leviathan. Please teach me how to live justly, to love Mercy and to walk humbly with You. I trust and declare Your weapons of warfare are powerful and effective in all things, including victory over Leviathan. I ask You to teach me through Your Word, through the power of the Holy Spirit and through my relationship with You how to live in Your Goodness and glory. Please teach me how to receive Your Goodness and glory in my life. Show me how to Love Your Goodness and glory. Please help me to live out Your Goodness and glory to impact the lives of those You have placed in my sphere of influence. Please speak to me through the power of the Holy Spirit and tell me Your truth. In Jesus' name, amen.

SESSION 12
Faith as Spiritual Warfare

Introduction

Hebrews 11:6:
But without faith it is impossible to please Him, for he who comes to God must believe that He is, and that He is a rewarder of those who diligently seek Him.

Questions Answered in This Session

- What is the definition of "Faith?"

- Faith opposes unbelief. What holds unbelief in place?

- When I believe and hold on to a promise given to me by God, how do I have Faith in Him and not make the promise an idol?

- What are the underlying strongholds in place that deceive us into thinking we are in Faith, when in reality we are making the promise an idol?

Definition of Faith

➤ **Definition of "faith"**—*pisits*—(Greek):
  1) "conviction of the truth of anything, belief; in the New Testament of a conviction or belief respecting man's relationship to God and divine things, generally with the included idea of trust and holy fervor born of faith and joined with it
     a) relating to God
        i) the conviction that God exists and is the creator and ruler of all things, the provider and bestower of eternal salvation through Christ
     b) relating to Christ
        i) strong and welcome conviction or belief that Jesus is the Messiah, through whom we obtain eternal salvation in the kingdom of God"

➤ **Definition of "rewarder"**—*misthapodotēs*—(Greek): "one who pays wages, a rewarder"

Hebrews 11:6 is the only time this word "rewarder" is mentioned in the New Testament.

Galatians 6:9 says to not "become weary in doing good for in due season we shall reap if we do not lose heart." God is Faithful to His Word. He *will* reward our Faith in Him.

This concept of God as a rewarder can be seen with the word "faithful," *pistos*, when Jesus told the Parable of the Talents (Matthew 25:14-30).

Faith: Spiritual Warfare Against Unbelief

How often have we doubted our Faith in God? We quote Mark 9:24 in prayer, "Lord I believe, help my unbelief!"

Since Faith opposes unbelief, when we battle unbelief, we need to have Faith. What keeps us from greater Faith?

First, unbelief is a stronghold with other like-minded strongholds keeping it in place.

Second, Faith is rooted in God. We need to live from His Faith—not from the faith we try to call upon from within ourselves. We need to see His example of Faithfulness to us and we need receive it from the Holy Spirit. As we experience this, we will understand true Faithfulness.

Where does unbelief reside?

- Unbelief resides in the mind, heart and emotions of a person.

Mark 11:22-24

- ➤ **Definition of "heart" (Greek):** "the soul or mind, as it is the fountain and seat of the thoughts, passions, desires, appetites, affections, purposes, endeavors"

- The soul comprises the mind, will and emotions.

- Belief resides not only in the mind and the will, but also in the heart and the emotions.

Deuteronomy 6:5:
"You shall love the LORD your God with all your heart, with all your soul, and with all your strength."

- ➤ **Definition of "heart" (Hebrew):** "heart; inner man, mind, will, heart, soul, understanding; mind, knowledge, thinking, reflection, memory; as seat of emotions and passions"

- ➢ **Definition of "soul" (Hebrew):** "soul, self, life, creature, person, appetite, mind, living being, desire, emotion, passion"

  <u>Mark 12:30</u>:
  "'And you shall love the L<small>ORD</small> *your God with all your heart, with all your soul, with all your mind, and with all your strength.' This is the first commandment."*

- ➢ **Definition of "heart" (Greek):** "the heart; the soul or mind, as it is the fountain and seat of the thoughts, passions, desires, appetites, affections, purposes, endeavours"

- ➢ **Definition of "soul" (Greek):** "the soul; the seat of the feelings, desires, affections, aversions (our heart, soul, etc.)"

Strongholds of Unbelief and Soul Wounds That Hold Unbelief in Place

- Orphan Spirit
- Spirit of Poverty
- Broken heart
- Dreams that have been delayed or stolen
- Broken relationships with earthly fathers that are not yet healed through relationship with Father God
- Pride
- Rebellion
- And many more

In essence, anything that comes in-between our relationship with God—anything that breaks down the relationship—can hold unbelief in place.

Faith:
Spiritual Warfare for Physical Healing and Freedom from Demonic Torment

John 14:12:
"Most assuredly, I say to you, he who believes in Me, the works that I do he will do also; and greater works than these he will do, because I go to My Father."

Matthew 8:8-13:
The centurion answered and said, "...But only speak a word, and my servant will be healed... When Jesus heard it, He marveled, and said to those who followed, "Assuredly, I say to you, I have not found such great faith, not even in Israel! ...Then Jesus said to the centurion, "Go your way; and as you have believed, so let it be done for you." And his servant was healed that same hour.

Matthew 15:22,28:
And behold, a woman of Canaan came from that region and cried out to Him, saying, "Have mercy on me, O Lord, Son of David! My daughter is severely demon-possessed...."

Then Jesus answered and said to her, "O woman, great is your faith! Let it be to you as you desire." And her daughter was healed from that very hour.

Matthew 10:7-8:
"And as you go, preach, saying, 'The kingdom of heaven is at hand.' Heal the sick, cleanse the lepers, raise the dead, cast out demons. Freely you have received, freely give."

Faith in Christ:
Spiritual Warfare for Miracles

Matthew 13:58:
He did not do many mighty works there because of their unbelief.

Matthew 8:5-13

Matthew 15:21-28

Faith Can Bring Blessings That Were Not Intended for Us

Gentile Mother

Matthew 15:21-28

King Hezekiah

2 Kings 20:1-6

Faith:
Spiritual Warfare for Peace

Romans 5:1-5:
Therefore, having been justified by faith, we have peace with God through our Lord Jesus Christ, through whom also we have access by faith into this grace in which we stand, and rejoice in hope of the glory of God. And not only that, but we also glory in tribulations, knowing that tribulation produces perseverance; and perseverance, character; and character, hope. Now hope does not disappoint, because the love of God has been poured out in our hearts by the Holy Spirit who was given to us.

Romans 5:1 shows we are justified through Faith. This Faith brings us into a righteous relationship with God through Jesus Christ.

This brings us into a covenant of Peace with the Father.

> **Definition of "peace"—*shalom*—(Hebrew):** "completeness, soundness, welfare, peace; completeness (in number); safety, soundness (in body); welfare, health, prosperity; peace, quiet, tranquility, contentment; peace, friendship of human relationships; peace friendship with God especially in covenant relationship; peace (from war) and peace (as adjective)"

Romans 5:2:
…through whom also we have access by faith into this grace in which we stand….

By Faith through Jesus Christ, we access grace.

> **Definition of "grace"—*charis*—(Greek):** "that which affords joy, pleasure, delight, sweetness, charm, loveliness: grace of speech."

Our Faith justifies us through Jesus Christ. We gain access to God through Faith in the grace by which we stand. In addition, we "rejoice in hope of the glory of God."

- ➢ **Definition of "glory"**—*doxa*—**(Greek):** "splendor, brightness, magnificence, excellence, and majesty"

Through Faith, we rejoice in the hope of God's splendor, brightness, magnificence, excellence and majesty.

Romans 5:3-4:
And not only that, but we also glory in tribulations, knowing that tribulation produces perseverance; and perseverance, character; and character, hope.

- ➢ **Definition of "glory" (Webster):** "to exult with joy; to rejoice"

We can employ Patience along with Joy to endure hardships and live in unity with our brothers and sisters.

Romans 5:5:
Now hope does not disappoint, because the love of God has been poured out in our hearts by the Holy Spirit who was given to us.

This brings us back to the Fruit of Love. He pours His Love into our hearts—not our minds.

Faith:
Spiritual Warfare as Reminder of
Utter Destruction of the Enemy

Philippians 1:27-28:
Only let your conduct be worthy of the gospel of Christ, so that whether I come and see you or am absent, I may hear of your affairs, that you stand fast in one spirit, with one mind striving together for the faith of the gospel, and not in any way terrified by your adversaries, which is to them a proof of perdition, but to you of salvation, and that of God.

1 John 4:4:
You are of God, little children, and have overcome them, because He who is in you is greater than he who is in the world.

The Greek word used here for "little children" is te*knion*. This is a diminutive of *teknon*, which means "child."

The word for "mature son" in the Greek is *huios*. In essence, the word *teknon* refers to a young child and to "being born into and begotten." When we enter the Kingdom of Heaven, we all enter as a *teknon*. It takes maturity to become a *huios*.

Jesus is not referred to in Scripture as *teknon*. He is referred to as *huios*.

Matthew 3:16-17:
When He had been baptized, Jesus came up immediately from the water; and behold, the heavens were opened to Him, and He saw the Spirit of God descending like a dove and alighting upon Him. And suddenly a voice came from heaven, saying, "This is My beloved Son [huios], in whom I am well pleased."

As soon as we are born into the family of God, we have access to victory over the Enemy.

Faith:
Spiritual Warfare Against the Spirit of Poverty

The Spirit of Poverty wants to keep us in lack of everything promised to us as our inheritance in Christ. It wants to prevent us from the abundance and overflow of the glorious riches that are ours through Faith. Through Faith, we have access to the wealth of God's Love. This spirit strives to keep us longing for Faith and Love, yet remain unfulfilled.

Ephesians 3:8-21:
To me, who am less than the least of all the saints, this grace was given, that I should preach among the Gentiles **the unsearchable riches of Christ, and to make all see what is the fellowship of the mystery, which from the beginning of the ages has been hidden in God who created all things through Jesus Christ; to the intent that now the manifold wisdom of God might be made known by the church to the principalities and powers in the heavenly places,** *according to the eternal purpose which He accomplished in Christ Jesus our Lord, in whom we have boldness and access with confidence through faith in Him. Therefore I ask that you do not lose heart at my tribulations for you, which is your glory.*

For this reason I bow my knees to the Father of our Lord Jesus Christ, from whom the whole family in heaven and earth is named, that He would grant you, according to the riches of His glory, to be strengthened with might through His Spirit in the inner man, **that Christ may dwell in your hearts through faith; that you, being rooted and grounded in love, may be able to comprehend with all the saints what** *is the width and length and depth and height—to know the love of Christ which passes knowledge; that you may be filled with all the fullness of God.*

Now to Him who is able to do exceedingly abundantly above all that we ask or think, according to the power that works in us, to Him be glory in the church by Christ Jesus to all generations, forever and ever. Amen. (Emphasis added.)

One purpose of the Spirit of Poverty is to keep us from seeking out the unsearchable riches of God's glory and to prevent the manifold wisdom of God to be made known by the Church to the principalities and powers in the heavenly places.

James 1:5-8

- **Definition of "manifold" (Webster):** "various in kind or quality; many in number; numerous; multiplied; complicated"[27]

Faith:
Belief in God vs. Turning His Promises into Idols

A stronghold that takes Faith in the promises of God and twists them into idols:

- Spirit of Poverty
  - We hold tight to the things we are given and are protective of them.

- Orphan Spirit
  - An Orphan Spirit does not allow us to know and understand the inheritance that is ours.

Things to know and understand to keep our promises in Faith and not turn them into idols:

- Know how justice, restoration and restitution work

- Live *from* Love, not *for* Love

- Live *from* eternity, not *for* eternity

- Live *from* the promise, not *for* the promise

- Do not make the promise according to our understanding

Isaiah 55:11:
"So shall My word be that goes forth from My mouth;
It shall not return to Me void,
But it shall accomplish what I please,
And it shall prosper in the thing for which I sent it."

Notes:

Prayers for Faith

Prayer to Break Unbelief

Dear Heavenly Father, in the name of the Lord Jesus Christ, thank You for Faith. Thank You for the example of Faith in the life of Your Son, Jesus Christ. I recognize I live with doubt and unbelief in my heart. Please show me any strongholds that keep unbelief in place. (Wait to see what the Holy Spirit tells you about this. You may want to write it down and pray to break it off if there is more than one item. For example, Spirit of Poverty, Religious Spirit, etc.) Lord, I thank You for revealing these strongholds that empower unbelief in my life. In the name of Jesus, I renounce agreement with these strongholds. Please forgive me, and I forgive myself. In the name of Jesus, I bind and break all of Satan's power and authority over me concerning these strongholds that hold doubt and unbelief in place. I ask You to forgive all my generations back to Adam and Eve and any participation they have had in these strongholds. I bind and break all generational curses these strongholds bring. Please heal my heart concerning these areas of wounding. Please heal my heart of the unbelief rooted in these strongholds. Please fill my entire being with Your Love. Please increase my Faith in You. Thank You for removing the unbelief from my heart and replacing it with Your Love and Your Faith. Show me how to be more relational with You in the areas of Faith and Love. May I live for You from my whole heart. I want to Love You with my heart, soul, mind and strength. In Jesus' name, amen.

Prayer for Healing of Soul Wounds and the Heart of Unbelief

Dear Heavenly Father, in the name of the Lord Jesus Christ, I ask You to please show me the wounds of my heart that hold unbelief in place. (Wait to see what the Holy Spirit tells you about this. You may want to write it down and pray to break it off. For example, broken relationships, broken promises by others, promises of God stolen by the Enemy, etc.) Thank You for being a God who delights in His relationship with me. Please forgive me for transferring onto You the characteristics of those in my life who have wounded my soul. Forgive me for accusing You of not being Good to me; my unbelief; and not having Faith in You because I placed greater faith in the pain that I suffered. In the name of the Lord Jesus Christ, I break agreement with the wounds, the pain, and the effect it has on my relationship with You. I break off all unbelief held in place because of the pain my heart holds in place. I break all of Satan's power and authority over me from these wounds that hold unbelief in place. I repent on behalf of all my generations of unbelief that is held in place due to broken promises by others toward my family. I renounce unbelief that occurred in my generations due to the Enemy stealing the promises meant for us. I break all generational curses resulting from unbelief, back to Adam and Eve. Please heal my soul—mind, will and emotions—with the power of Your Holy Spirit. Please fill my entire being with Your perfect Love. Please show me Your true nature and character so I may grow in understanding and experience of Your Love and Goodness to me. Please impart to me Your Faith. Holy Spirit, please release Faith in me and teach me how to live in Faith essential for healings, miracles, signs, wonders, raising the dead, cleansing the lepers, casting out demons, reminding the Enemy of his destruction, and bringing blessings into my life that may not necessarily be intended for me. In Jesus' name, amen.

Prayer to Renounce Unbelief

Dear Heavenly Father, in the name of the Lord Jesus Christ, please show me anything I have said or done that is in agreement with unbelief. (Wait to see what the Holy Spirit tells you about this. You may want to write it down and pray to break it off. Example, it may be an oath to an occult group, agreement with a denomination's doctrine that contains unbelief in it, a declaration of not ever trusting God because of a painful event, etc.) I recognize that my agreement with unbelief is sin. Please forgive me for this agreement with unbelief. I forgive myself. In the name of Jesus, I bind and break all of Satan's power and authority in my agreement with unbelief. Please fill my heart with the power of the Holy Spirit to heal me of unbelief and fill my entire being with Your Love that passes understanding. In Jesus' name, amen.

(At this point, you may want to take some time soaking in the Love of God and in the power of the Holy Spirit to heal your soul of the wounds that you just prayed about. Return to soaking in His Love and in the power of the Holy Spirit in days and weeks to come, as needed. Some wounds are very deep and require more time for healing. Remember, the place of Faith is in your heart. Therefore, your heart needs to be healed of the wounds that hold unbelief in place.)

Prayer to Overcome Spirit of Poverty with Faith

Dear Heavenly Father, in the name of the Lord Jesus Christ, I recognize I have agreed with the Spirit of Poverty in my life and allowed it to steal my Faith and Love in You. This is sin, and I repent. Please forgive me for agreeing with the Spirit of Poverty. I forgive myself. In the name of Jesus, I bind and break the power of the Spirit of Poverty over my life relating to receiving Your Love, maintaining Faith in You and receiving Your manifold wisdom (add any other areas the Holy Spirit brings to your mind). I ask You to bring justice to me regarding all that has been stolen in my life due to unbelief. Please restore and bring into my life the restitution of the things stolen, killed and destroyed by the Spirit of Poverty and a lack of belief. Please bring into my life an abundance of Your Love so that my heart will be filled with Faith in You. Show me Your Goodness, which includes abundance. Remove the Spirit of Poverty from my life. It is the opposite of Your abundance. I no longer give it permission to steal from me. I am Your child and I thank You for Your abundance, Goodness and Love. Thank You for the Holy Spirit who can give me Faith to fill my heart with belief in You. Please heal my soul—mind, will and emotions—from the poverty mindset. Rewire my mind to think from the Kingdom perspective of Your Love, abundance and Goodness for my life. In Jesus' name, amen.

Prayer to Repent for Turning God's Promises Into Idols

Dear Heavenly Father, in the name of the Lord Jesus Christ, please forgive me for making an idol of the promise that (fill in the promise the Lord made you). I recognize I have sinned in crossing the line from believing You will fulfill the promise to making it an idol. I repent of the Orphan Spirit, the Spirit of Poverty and the unbelief that You will be true to Your promise. I repent for receiving the promise in my understanding and holding on to it so tightly that my focus was on the promise and not on my relationship with You. Please forgive me. I forgive myself. I repent and ask for forgiveness of my generations back to Adam and Eve for taking Your promises and turning them into idols. I bind and break all of Satan's power and authority off of me and my generations in this issue. I choose to change the way I think about Your promises. I thank You for Your justice, restoration and restitution for the times the promises were stolen by the Enemy. I rest in the promises yet to come. I declare that You are Faithful. If the promises are stolen, You are a good and faithful Judge and You will bring about justice. I choose to live from Your Love and not for it. I do not need to earn Your Love, but can live from it. I choose to live from the abundance of eternity and not strive for it. I choose not to twist the promise and make it live up to my understanding. Holy Spirit, please come and teach me more about how to live from the promises of God and not for them, how to believe in Faith they will come to fulfillment, and not to make idols of them. In Jesus' name, amen.

SESSION 13
Gentleness as Spiritual Warfare

__Gentleness__

"There is scarcely any other virtue which the demons fear as much as gentleness (meekness)." Evagrios the Solitary (c. A.D. 345-399)[28]

> **Definition of "gentleness" (Hebrew and Greek):** "humility and meekness"

> **Definition of "humility" (Webster):** "humble—not proud, haughty, arrogant, or assertive"[29]

> **Antonym of gentleness:** "roughness"[30]

> **Synonyms of roughness:** "brusqueness, violence, vagueness and rudeness"[31]

Satan's Opposition to Gentleness

Bitterness and Anger:

1. Unforgiveness
2. Resentment
3. Retaliation
4. Anger
5. Hatred
6. Violence
7. Murder

Vagueness; passive-aggressive behavior

> **Definition of "meek"**—*praus*—**(Greek):** "power under control"

Example of Moses' Meekness

Notes:

Example of Jesus' Meekness

Jesus and the Money Changers

Mark 11:11-13, 15-19:
And Jesus went into Jerusalem and into the temple. So when He had looked around at all things, as the hour was already late, He went out to Bethany with the twelve.

Now the next day, when they had come out from Bethany...[the story of the fig tree].

So they came to Jerusalem. Then Jesus went into the temple and began to drive out those who bought and sold in the temple, and overturned the tables of the money changers and the seats of those who sold doves. And He would not allow anyone to carry wares through the temple. Then He taught, saying to them, "Is it not written, 'My house shall be called a house of prayer for all nations'? But you have made it a 'den of thieves.' "

And the scribes and chief priests heard it and sought how they might destroy Him; for they feared Him, because all the people were astonished at His teaching. When evening had come, He went out of the city.

John 5:19:
Then Jesus answered and said to them, "Most assuredly, I say to you, the Son can do nothing of Himself, but what He sees the Father do; for whatever He does, the Son also does in like manner.

Humility Focuses on Relationship Rather Than the Need to be Right

Philippians 2:5-8:
Let this mind be in you which was also in Christ Jesus, who, being in the form of God, did not consider it robbery to be equal with God, but made Himself of no reputation, taking the form of a bondservant, and coming in the likeness of men. And being found in appearance as a man, He humbled Himself and became obedient to the point of death, even the death of the cross.

Notes:

Gentleness Imparts Greatness

Psalm 18:35:
*You have also given me the shield of Your salvation;
Your right hand has held me up,
Your gentleness has made me great.*

2 Samuel 22:36:
*"You have also given me the shield of Your salvation;
Your gentleness has made me great."*

➤ **Definition of "great" (Hebrew):** "be or become great, be or become many, be or become much, be or become numerous; to make much, make many, have many; to increase greatly or exceedingly; to make great, enlarge, do much"

Psalm 18:29-36:
*For by You I can run against a troop,
By my God I can leap over a wall.
As for God, His way is perfect;
The word of the LORD is proven;
He is a shield to all who trust in Him.*

*For who is God, except the LORD?
And who is a rock, except our God?
It is God who arms me with strength,
And makes my way perfect.
He makes my feet like the feet of deer,
And sets me on my high places.
He teaches my hands to make war,
So that my arms can bend a bow of bronze.*

*You have also given me the shield of Your salvation;
Your right hand has held me up,
Your gentleness has made me great.
You enlarged my path under me,
So my feet did not slip.*

Matthew 6:33:
"But seek first the kingdom of God and His righteousness, and all these things shall be added to you."

Isaiah 43:25:
[Thus says the LORD] "I, even I, am He who blots out your transgressions for My own sake; And I will not remember your sins."

Gentleness:
Spiritual Warfare Against Anger and Pride

Lucifer and Anger

Ezekiel 28:16:
"By the abundance of your trading
You became filled with violence within,
And you sinned;
Therefore I cast you as a profane thing out of the mountain of God;
And I destroyed you, O covering cherub,
From the midst of the fiery stones."

Lucifer and Pride

Isaiah 14:13-17:
"For you have said in your heart:
'I will ascend into heaven,
I will exalt my throne above the stars of God;
I will also sit on the mount of the congregation
On the farthest sides of the north;
I will ascend above the heights of the clouds,
I will be like the Most High.'
Yet you shall be brought down to Sheol,
To the lowest depths of the Pit.

"Those who see you will gaze at you,
And consider you, saying:
'Is this the man who made the earth tremble,
Who shook kingdoms,
Who made the world as a wilderness
And destroyed its cities,
Who did not open the house of his prisoners?'"

Notes:

Gentleness:
Spiritual Warfare Against Self-Hatred and Unloving

Self-sabotage rooted in self-hatred undermines greatness.

Notes:

Gentleness:
Spiritual Warfare for Correction and Restoration

2 Timothy 2:23-26:
*But avoid foolish and ignorant disputes, knowing that they generate strife. And a servant of the Lord must not quarrel but be **gentle** to all, able to teach, **patient**, in humility correcting those who are in opposition, if God perhaps will grant them repentance, so that they may know the truth, and that they may come to their senses and escape the snare of the devil, having been taken captive by him to do his will.* (Emphasis added.)

Gentleness:
Spiritual Warfare for Coming into Our Inheritance

Psalm 37:11:
*But the meek shall inherit the earth,
And shall delight themselves in the abundance of peace.*

Matthew 5:5:
*"Blessed are the meek,
For they shall inherit the earth."*

How Does Gentleness Lead Us to Our Inheritance?

> **Definition of "inherit" (Hebrew):** "to seize, to take possession of, inherit, occupy and to be an heir"

Inheritance and Sonship

Inheritance is obtained by rights as an heir through sonship.

Romans 8:16-17:
The Spirit Himself bears witness with our spirit that we are children of God, and if children, then heirs—heirs of God and joint heirs with Christ, if indeed we suffer with Him, that we may also be glorified together.

> **Definition of "earth" (Hebrew and Greek):** "the land, the earth as a whole, the earth as opposed to the heaven, and the inhabited earth, including the abode of men and animal"

How and when do we come into this inheritance?

Hebrews 9:15-18, 22 (NIV):
For this reason Christ is the mediator of a new covenant, that those who are called may receive the promised eternal inheritance—now that he has died as a ransom to set them free from the sins committed under the first covenant.

In the case of a will, it is necessary to prove the death of the one who made it, because a will is in force only when somebody has died; it never takes effect while the one who made it is living. This is why even the first covenant was not put into effect without blood....In fact, the law requires that nearly everything be cleansed with blood, and without the shedding of blood there is no forgiveness.

Gentleness:
Spiritual Warfare for Protecting the Family

Role of Mothers and Gentleness

1. Comfort

2. Nurture

3. Teach

Underestimating the Importance of Gentleness

Any lack in men's understanding of and living in Gentleness is a direct attack against families as men are the family's first line of defense.

Role of Fathers and Gentleness

It is important for men to understand Gentleness in the role of the family. Gentleness leads to greatness and correlates to identity and inheritance.

1. Protection

2. Provision

3. Identity

Gentleness:
Spiritual Warfare Against the Spirit of Poverty

Satan uses the Spirit of Poverty as a strong weapon to keep the Church powerless and ineffective. This spirit is obviously connected to finances, but it is more than financial poverty.

> **John 10:10:**
> *"The thief comes only to steal and kill and destroy; I have come that they may have life, and have it to the full."*

> ➤ **Definition of "poverty" (Isaacs):** "living in lack, living without something that is established for us through the finished work of the Cross, and experiencing

anything that is less than the fullness of our inheritance in Jesus Christ through the power of the Holy Spirit. This includes, but is not limited to, health, creativity, finances, mind, emotions, etc."

Gentleness Is Strategic in Overcoming the Spirit of Poverty

Poverty is warfare against greatness and inheritance.

Not tithing (Malachi), stealing, gambling, fraud, etc., give legal access to the Spirit of Poverty. It is essential to repent of these sins to end the legal access the Enemy has to curse us.

Is Poverty Demonic?

John 10:10

Spiritual Abundance

Ephesians 3:14-21:
*For this reason I bow my knees to the Father of our Lord Jesus Christ, from whom the whole family in heaven and earth is named, that He would grant you, according to the **riches of His glory**, **to be strengthened with might through His Spirit in the inner man, that Christ may dwell in your hearts through faith;** that you, **being rooted and grounded in love**, may be able to comprehend with all the saints what is the **width and length and depth and height—to know the love of Christ which passes knowledge; that you may be filled with all the fullness of God**.*

Now to Him who is able to do exceedingly abundantly above all that we ask or think, according to the power that works in us, to Him be glory in the church by Christ Jesus to all generations, forever and ever. Amen. (Emphasis added.)

Physical and External Abundance

Philippians 4:19:
And my God shall supply all your need according to His riches in glory by Christ Jesus.

- ➤ **Definition of "riches" (Greek):** "abundance of external possession; fullness, abundance, plentitude; a good that with which one is enriched"

Matthew 6:33:
But seek first the kingdom of God and His righteousness, and all these things shall be added to you.

How Do We Act in Gentleness?

Take care of strongholds of bitterness and everything that leads to selfish ambition.

This opens us to the gifts of Love and Gentleness.

Gentleness replaces bitterness and self-hatred. Gentleness is God's positive counterpoint to the bitterness of Satan.

Gentleness is an issue of the heart and not solely relegated to the mind.

What does living with Gentleness look like?

- Repentance
- Replacing
- Relationship
- Questions and Conversation
- Receiving from Father God

Notes:

Prayers for Gentleness

Prayer of Repentance for Anger and Impartation of Gentleness

Dear Heavenly Father, in the name of the Lord Jesus Christ, I recognize the areas in which I have been angry toward (list the person or people here, including ways you have not forgiven yourself). I repent of this anger and change the way I think about anger and unforgiveness. I bind and break Satan's power and authority over me in the area of anger in my life. I repent of anger in my generations back to Adam and Eve. I bind and break Satan's power and authority over the area of anger in all my generations. I renounce agreement with anger.

I repent of the ways I have undermined my greatness in You because of anger toward myself and others. I repent of the ways my generations back to Adam and Eve have undermined greatness from You because of anger toward ourselves or others. I choose to embrace Your Gentleness and renounce unforgiveness and anger. I bind and break all of Satan's power and authority in my life and in all my generations in the area of anger and undermining the greatness You have for me.

Heavenly Father, please place Your Gentleness in me. Remove all aspects of bitterness—unforgiveness, resentment, retaliation, anger, hatred, violence and murder—from me and replace bitterness with Your Perfect Love and character of Gentleness. Please teach me through Your Word, through the Holy Spirit and through intimacy with You how to live with the character of one who is truly Gentle. Renew my thinking and my heart to respond in Love and forgiveness and see others with Your eyes and with Your heart. I receive Your Gentleness and declare it is Your Gentleness that makes me great. I declare that being made in Your image, I will live in Your Gentleness with a focus to impart greatness to others. Please bring about justice, restoration and restitution in the areas of Gentleness and greatness that have been stolen from me by the Enemy. In Jesus' name, amen.

Prayer of Repentance for Pride and Impartation of Gentleness and Humility

Dear Heavenly Father, in the name of the Lord Jesus Christ, I recognize the areas in which I have been prideful and have taken the stance that being right is more important than my relationships. I repent of this pride and change the way I think about it. Going back to Adam and Eve and through all my generations, I repent of pride and putting the need to be right over focusing on the best interest of relationships. Father, please forgive me of my pride. I bind and break Satan's power and authority over the area of pride in my life and my generations. I renounce agreement with pride.

I repent of the ways I have undermined my humility and inheritance in You because of pride. I repent of the ways my generations back to Adam and Eve have undermined our inheritance from You because of pride. I choose to embrace your Gentleness and Humility and renounce focusing on the pride of being right. I bind and break all of Satan's power and authority in my life and in all my generations in the area of pride, which undermine my inheritance in You.

Heavenly Father, please place in me Your Gentleness. Remove all aspects of pride from me and replace it with Your perfect Love and character of Gentleness. Please teach me through Your Word, through the Holy Spirit and through intimacy with You how to live with the character of one who is truly Gentle and Humble. Thank You that Jesus was Humble and put greater importance on relationship with me than on His reputation and His righteousness. Please teach me how to be a recipient of this Humility and Mercy. Renew my thinking and my heart to respond in Love and Humility and see others with Your eyes and with Your heart. I receive Your Gentleness and Humility. Please teach me to be a good steward of the inheritance You have for me. Father, please bring about justice, restoration and restitution in the areas of Gentleness, Humility and inheritance that have been stolen from me and my generations by the Enemy. In Jesus' name, amen.

Prayer to Break the Spirit of Poverty

Dear Heavenly Father, in the name of the Lord Jesus Christ, please forgive me and my ancestors for any time we have robbed You by not bringing the full tithe into Your storehouse, thus establishing legal right to be cursed. Please forgive me and my ancestors for any time we have gambled, stolen, committed fraud, embezzled, swindled, counterfeited, been bad stewards or involved in piracy, and any other ways in which we disobeyed Your law and established legal access for the Enemy to steal, kill and destroy our family.

I repent of believing the lie that poverty is holiness and/or declaring and believing that anything less than abundance is acceptable. In doing so, I called You and Your Son a liar when He declared that He brings abundance to my life. Forgive me for my unbelief and the curses it spawned, relating to—but not limited to—creativity, resources, opportunities, finances, dreams, areas of influence, friends, health, holiness, spiritual gifts and fruit.

I bind and break Satan's power and authority over me in these areas of my life and in all my generations back to Adam and Eve. I declare in the name of Jesus, that all curses associated with these sins be broken in my life and in all my generations in the name of Jesus.

I ask You, through the power of Your Holy Spirit, to replace these curses with the blessings of Your Gentleness, which include greatness, inheritance, abundance, protection and restored identity. Please renew within me the dreams and desires You have foreordained for me. I receive them. I choose to align myself with Your nature and declare with the Psalmist, "Your Gentleness has made me great." In Jesus' name, amen.

SESSION 14
Self-Control as Spiritual Warfare

Introduction

2 Corinthians 10:1-5

First, we need to break the things that hold us in bondage. Then we can take our thoughts captive.

Steps to Bondage (Refresher from Session 1)
Step 1: Temptation (dwelling on this leads to step 2)
Step 2: Sinning and practicing the act (repenting goes up to step 1, continuing leads to step 3)
Step 3: Habit (repenting goes up to step 2, continuing leads to step 4)
Step 4: Bondage (repenting goes up to step 3, continuing remains at step 4)

Self-Control as Spiritual Warfare

Self-Control is necessary because of free will.

- Lucifer

- Adam and Eve

Self-Control is warfare against many things, some of which are cheating; stealing; impulsiveness; responding in anger and retaliation; sexual sins; lying; gossip; slander; murder; overeating; and over-spending of time, money and resources.

Self-Control summarizes of the Fruit of the Holy Spirit and must be based in Love to come to its fullest expression and effectiveness. Love is the basis and the foundation of all of the Fruit of the Holy Spirit, while Self-Control is the ability to apply the Fruit of the Holy Spirit to build up the strength we have in the Lord. After we apply it in our lives, it extends out to those in our spheres of influence.

Self-Control:
Spiritual Warfare Against "As in the Days of Noah"

2 Timothy 3:1-5:
But know this, that in the last days perilous times will come: For men will be lovers of themselves, lovers of money, boasters, proud, blasphemers, disobedient to parents, unthankful, unholy, unloving, unforgiving, slanderers, without self-control, brutal, despisers of good, traitors, headstrong, haughty, lovers of pleasure rather than lovers of God, having a form of godliness but denying its power. And from such people turn away!

Scripture lists characteristics of what people will be like in the last days, which includes a lack of Self-Control.

Luke 17:26-30

History of the Nephilim Before the Flood

Enoch describes how the Watcher Angels fell into corruption in Enoch 6:1-8.

Genesis 6:1-8:
Now it came to pass, when men began to multiply on the face of the earth, and daughters were born to them, that the sons of God saw the daughters of men, that they were beautiful; and they took wives for themselves of all whom they chose.

And the LORD said, "My Spirit shall not strive with man forever, for he is indeed flesh; yet his days shall be one hundred and twenty years." There were giants on the earth in those days, and also afterward, when the sons of God came in to the daughters of men and they bore children to them. Those were the mighty men who were of old, men of renown.

Then the LORD saw that the wickedness of man was great in the earth, and that every intent of the thoughts of his heart was only evil continually. And the LORD was sorry that He had made man on the earth, and He was grieved in His heart. So the LORD said, "I will destroy man whom I have created from the face of the earth, both man and beast, creeping thing and birds of the air, for I am sorry that I have made them." But Noah found grace in the eyes of the LORD.

Genesis states that giants lived on the earth prior to the flood and afterward. What happened that allowed the giants to reappear after the flood?

History of the Nephilim After the Flood

Noah and His Family

Genesis 9:18-25

Ham's Descendants and the Nephilim

Genesis 10:6 (NIV):
The sons of Ham: Cush, Egypt, Put, and Canaan.

Genesis 10:7-12

Ham's Firstborn Son Cush

Cush fathered Nimrod.

Genesis 10:8:
Cush begot Nimrod; he began to be a mighty one on the earth.

- **Definition for "mighty one" (Hebrew):** "strong, mighty"
  - This phrase used in reference to Nimrod is the same as that used in Genesis 6:4 when describing the Nephilim as the mighty men of old, the men of renown.

Through choices of his own, Nimrod began the process to become a Nephilim. This established giants living on earth after the flood.

Nimrod's kingdoms included Babel (Genesis 10:10, Genesis 11:1-9) and Nineveh (Genesis 10:11).

Jonah 1:2

Ham's Son Mizraim

Through Ham's son Mizraim came the Philistines, a main enemy of the Israelites when they entered into the Promised Land after the exodus from Egypt. An infamous warrior was the giant Goliath, whom David killed (1 Samuel 17).

Genesis 10:13-14

Ham's Son Canaan

Throughout Canaan, the descendants spread through what later became known as the Promised Land.

Genesis 10:15-19

Abraham inherited the land of Canaan, settling there in obedience to the Lord's promise (Genesis 12-13). Abraham interceded on behalf of Sodom and Gomorrah before the Lord destroyed them (Genesis 18-19).

Exodus 3:8

The Jebusites, Amorites, Gergashites and Hivites were some of the nations that the Israelites fought when they took the Promised Land.

Connection of Jesus' Reference to the Days of Noah and Self-Control

In Luke 17:26-30, Jesus refers to the end times as the days of Noah. He also refers to the days of Lot.

Jude connects the Watcher Angels from the days of Noah and the days of Lot in the context of a lack of self-control.

Jude 1:6-8:
And the angels who did not keep their proper domain, but left their own abode, He has reserved in everlasting chains under darkness for the judgment of the great day; as Sodom and Gomorrah, and the cities around them in a similar manner to these, having given themselves over to sexual immorality and gone after strange flesh, are set forth as an example, suffering the vengeance of eternal fire.

Self-Control is a powerful weapon against the warfare of the Enemy.

If the end times are like the days of Noah, then we can exercise Self-Control in our lives to war against the evil that results from a lack of Self-Control.

Self-Control:
Spiritual Warfare Against Spirit of Poverty

We live in a time where the culture is based on instant gratification.

When we are in debt we have an inability to act from a position of authority in the Lord and the provision that comes from one who is in a position of royalty.

Proverbs 22:7:
The rich rules over the poor,
And the borrower is servant to the lender.

What Are Some Causes for Indebtedness?

- Impulse spending

- Instant gratification

- Not tithing

- Generational curses

    ### Malachi 3:8-12:
    "Will a man rob God?
    Yet you have robbed Me!
    But you say,
    'In what way have we robbed You?'
    In tithes and offerings.
    You are cursed with a curse,
    For you have robbed Me,
    Even this whole nation.
    Bring all the tithes into the storehouse,
    That there may be food in My house,
    And try Me now in this," Says the LORD of hosts,
    "If I will not open for you the windows of heaven
    And pour out for you such blessing
    That there will not be room enough to receive it.

    "And I will rebuke the devourer for your sakes,
    So that he will not destroy the fruit of your ground,
    Nor shall the vine fail to bear fruit for you in the field,"
    Says the LORD of hosts;
    "And all nations will call you blessed,
    For you will be a delightful land,"
    Says the LORD of hosts.

The Enemy wants to have people believe they cannot live on less than what they earn. On the contrary, not tithing locks a person into a curse on himself and his descendants.

It is vital to break the curse of the Spirit of Poverty. We need to live in abundance so we may bring the Kingdom of Heaven to earth.

Prayers for Self-Control

Prayer to Break Areas of Bondages

Dear Heavenly Father, in the name of the Lord Jesus Christ, I recognize I have sinned by (name the area of bondage, such as sexual sins, pornography, gambling, compulsive shopping, etc.). I take responsibility for (list the sin here) and I repent. Please forgive me, and I forgive myself. I renounce agreement with this sin and I choose to change the way I think about it. Please forgive my generations back to Adam and Eve on both side of my family line for any sin committed in these areas. I bind and break all of Satan's power and authority over me in my generations in the area of this sin. Through the power of the Holy Spirit, please replace these bondages with Your Love, Joy, Peace, Gentleness and Self-Control. Please teach me through Your Word, through the Holy Spirit and through intimacy with You how to live in complete freedom and how to live righteously. Through the power of the Holy Spirit and through Your glory, please heal me completely from the effects of this sin in my body, mind, thoughts, will, heart, emotions, passions and desires. In Jesus' name, amen.

Prayer for Repentance of Lack of Self-Control and Impartation of Self-Control

Dear Heavenly Father, in the name of the Lord Jesus Christ, I recognize I have sinned by giving in to a lack of Self-Control. I take responsibility for all the times I have not acted in Self-Control (list the specific areas and times you have not acted in Self-Control). I repent from these and I turn from them. Please forgive me for these instances in which I have not demonstrated Self-Control. I bind and break any and all of Satan's power and authority over me in the area of not acting with Self-Control. I forgive and release myself from all sins committed by not exercising Self-Control. Father, please send the power of Your Holy Spirit to fill my life and to empower me to live a Self-Controlled life as demonstrated to us by Your Son, Jesus Christ. Please fill me with Your Joy that I may be righteous and victorious in this area of my life, that I may live the fullness of righteousness and freedom You have destined me to live. Father, I give You this area of the lack of Self-Control in my life and ask You to replace it. Holy Spirit, what do You wish to say to me about this area of my life? In Jesus' name, amen.

Prayer to Break the Curse of the Spirit of Poverty

Dear Heavenly Father, I recognize I have sinned by not being a good steward of the money and the resources You have entrusted to me. I repent and change the way I think about the money You have trusted me to use for Your Kingdom. Please forgive me, for the following:
- for not tithing;
- for believing the lie that You cannot be trusted to provide for me if I tithe;
- for not believing that You will provide;
- for buying and charging items that I did not have the money for;
- for not being a good steward of the money You have given me (list specifics);
- and for giving money to the occult knowingly or unknowingly. (Add any other items that the Holy Spirit brings to mind that you need to repent of in your use of money.)

I repent on behalf of my family for any time my generations did not tithe and any time they gave money to the occult. (List anything else the Holy Spirit brings to mind.) Heavenly Father, please forgive me and my generations for misuse of money. I forgive myself and my family for any ways we have not been proper stewards of the money entrusted to us. I bind and break Satan's power and authority over me in any curses I brought on myself or that my ancestors brought on themselves and on me when we robbed You by misusing money and not tithing. Father, please restore to me that which has been lost and stolen during this process. Please teach me to be a good steward of my money. Show me Your provision in my life. I choose to trust You with my money. I choose to trust You to provide for me. You are a better provider for me and my family than I am. May I learn and apply these principles so that I may be a blessing to a greater sphere of influence. Please teach me what it is to truly be a son or a daughter in Your Kingdom and to know how to distribute the resources of the Kingdom in accordance with Your wisdom and Your heart. In Jesus' name, amen.

Notes

[1] All Bible verses are from the New King James Version unless otherwise referenced.

Any time a word is defined and referenced, and it is the English word translated from the Hebrew or Greek, its Hebrew or Greek definition is found at www.blueletterbible.org, which references Strong's Concordance.

Words used in reference to God are capitalized. This includes pronouns and when the individual Fruit of the Holy Spirit refers to the nature and character of God. No changes to capitalization are applied to Scripture verses. Thus, the capitalization is the preference of the publishers of the particular translation.

Prayers at the end of each section of this study guide have been edited since the recording of the CD/DVD series. The integrity of the prayers remains intact.

It is intended that any discrepancies of Scripture, Scripture reference, Strong's Concordance references, etc. in the CD/DVD recordings are correct in the written form of this study guide.

[2] James Logan, Biblical Restoration Ministries, "How We Can Help Others," accessed 24 October 2013. www.biblicalrestorationministries.org/how_we_can_help_others_%28VIDEO%29.html

[3] *Sozo*, DVD, Dawna Desilva and Teresa Liebscher (2009; Redding, CA: Sound Wisdom/Bethel Church).

[4] Caroline Leaf, *The Gift in You*, (Southlake: Inprov, Ltd., 2009), 143.

[5] Hebrew Interlinear Bible, "Ruth 2:3," accessed 22 March 2014. www.scripture4all.org/OnlineInterlinear/OTpdf/rut2.pdf

[6] His Dwelling Place, *The Arsenal*, (2007), 9.

[7] His Dwelling Place, *The Arsenal*, (2007), 7.

[8] Rick Joyner, *Overcoming the Religious Spirit*, (Charlotte: MorningStar Publications, 1998), 7.

[9] Wikipedia, "Word Search for Legalism," Wikipedia The Free Encyclopedia, accessed 24 October 2013. en.wikipedia.org/wiki/Legalism_(theology).

[10] Webster's 1828 Dictionary, "Dictionary Search for Jealousy," accessed 24 October 2013. 1828.mshaffer.com/d/word/jealousy.

[11] His Dwelling Place, *The Arsenal*, (2007), 5.

[12] Webster's 1828 Dictionary, "Dictionary Search for Doubt," accessed 7 January 2013. www.webstersdictionary1828.com/Dictionary/doubt.

[13] Wikipedia, "Word Search for Doubt," Wikipedia The Free Encyclopedia, accessed 7 January 2013. en.wikipedia.org/wiki/Doubt.

[14] Merriam-Webster, "Dictionary Search for Joy," accessed 29 January 2013. www.merriam-webster.com/dictionary/joy.

[15] Merriam-Webster, "Dictionary Search for Glad," accessed 29 January 2013. www.merriam-webster.com/dictionary/glad.

[16]Ira Milligan, *Understanding the Dreams you Dream*, (Shippensburg: Treasure House, 1997), 93. Rick Joyner, *Overcoming the Religious Spirit*, (Charlotte: MorningStar Publications, 1998), 7.

[17]Merriam-Webster, "Dictionary Search for Gospel," accessed 9 April 2013. www.merriam-webster.com/dictionary/gospel.

[18]Hebrew Interlinear Bible, "Ruth 2:3," accessed 22 March 2014. www.scripture4all.org/OnlineInterlinear/OTpdf/rut2.pdf.

[19]Merriam-Webster, "Dictionary Search for Beckon," accessed 13 January 2013. www.merriam-webster.com/dictionary/beckon.

[20]Merriam-Webster, "Dictionary Search for Sate," accessed 13 January 2013. www.merriam-webster.com/dictionary/sate.

[21]Merriam-Webster, "Dictionary Search for Surfeit," accessed 13 January 2013. www.merriam-webster.com/dictionary/surfeit.

[22]Merriam-Webster, "Dictionary Search for Satisfy," accessed 13 January 2013. www.merriam-webster.com/dictionary/satisfy.

[23]Arthur Burk, *The Redemptive Gifts of Individuals*. Sapphire Leadership Group. CD. 2000.

[24]Rick Joyner, *Overcoming the Religious Spirit*, (Charlotte: MorningStar Publications, 1998), 7.

[25]Step Into Dressage, accessed 15 September 2012 www.stepintodressage.com/double.html.

[26]Webster's 1828 Dictionary, "Dictionary Search for Doubt," accessed 7 January 2013. 1828.mshaffer.com/d/search/word,eat.

[27]Webster's 1918 Dictionary, "Manifold" www.webster-dictionary.org/definition/manifold (accessed January 26, 2012).

[28]G.E.H. Palmer, et al., trans., *The Philokalia: The Complete Text* (Vol. 1), (London: Faber and Faber, 1979), 46.

[29]Merriam-Webster, "Dictionary Search for Humble," accessed 24 October 2013. www.merriam-webster.com/dictionary/humble.

[30]"Gentleness," Encarta Dictionary 2008.

[31]"Roughness," Encarta Dictionary 2008.

www.ingramcontent.com/pod-product-compliance
Lightning Source LLC
Chambersburg PA
CBHW081236170426
43198CB00017B/2777